The wearing of the black

The wearing of the black

An anthology of contemporary Ulster poetry

Edited by Padraic Fiacc

Blackstaff Press   Belfast

© Introduction by Padraic Fiacc 1974
© This collection by Blackstaff Press Limited 1974

All rights reserved. No part of this publication may be reproduced, stored in a retrieval system, or transmitted, in any form or by any means, electronic, mechanical, photocopying, recording or otherwise, without the prior permission of Blackstaff Press Limited.

Published by Blackstaff Press Limited, 16 Donegall Square South, Belfast BT1 5JF, with the assistance of the Arts Council of Northern Ireland.

For Aunt Mary

SBN 85640 069 6

Conditions of Sale - This book shall not without the written consent of the Publishers first given be lent, re-sold, hired out or otherwise disposed of by way of trade in any form of binding or cover other than that in which it is published.

Printed in Northern Ireland by Belfast Litho Printers Limited.

Contents

Acknowledgements	vi
Introduction	vii
First movement: prologues	1
Second movement: Derry	41
Third movement: Belfast	79
Fourth movement: epilogues	117
Biographies and index to poets	159
Index to titles and first lines	170

Acknowledgements

Grateful acknowledgement is made to Carcanet Press Ltd for permission to reprint 'Under a Cloud' and 'Revolutionary Revolution' from *Minute Book of a City* by George Buchanan (©George Buchanan); to Faber & Faber Ltd for permission to reprint 'The Field Hospital' and 'The Indians on Alcatraz' from *New Weather* by Paul Muldoon, 'Docker' from *Death of a Naturalist* by Seamus Heaney, and 'The Tollund Man' and 'The Other Side' from *Wintering Out* by Seamus Heaney; to Gill & Macmillan Ltd for permission to reprint 'The Raid', 'Belfast 1964' and 'English Class' by Conleth Ellis from *Under The Stone*; to Victor Gollancz Ltd for permission to reprint 'A Soldier's Son' and 'Child of Our Time' from *The War Horse* by Eavan Boland, and 'Letter to Derek Mahon', 'Letter to Seamus Heaney', 'Wounds', 'Nightmare' and 'Kindertotenlieder' from *An Exploded View* by Michael Longley; to Martin, Brian and O'Keefe Ltd for permission to reprint 'Meditations on the Suspension of Stormont' and 'Children's Games' from *This Hardening Ground* by Shaun Traynor; to the Marvell Press for permission to reprint 'Derry Images, 1968-71', 'Summer 1970' and 'An Ulster Garland' from *Living Room* by Andrew Waterman, and to Oxford University Press for permission to reprint 'The Bullaun' and 'Please Identify Yourself' from *The Scenic Route* by Fleur Adcock (© Oxford University Press 1974), 'Ecclesiastes', 'Edvard Munch', 'As It Should Be' and 'Rage for Order' from *Lives* by Derek Mahon (© Oxford University Press 1972) and 'Glengormley' from *Night Crossing* by Derek Mahon (© Oxford University Press 1968).

For permission to reprint the extract on the cover of this book from *Poems* by Wilfred Owen, edited by Siegfried Sassoon, the publishers thank the executors of the estate of Harold Owen and Chatto & Windus Ltd.

Introduction

This anthology, which has been prepared at a certain time - 1974 - in a certain place - Northern Ireland - does not pretend to offer any final statement on such general questions as how deeply contemporary violence can enter a poet's inner being, or how far it should be allowed to do so by the poet himself. Rather it merely poses the question by presenting poets touched by, or involved in, the situation here, and suggests how they have tried to come to terms with it in their poetry. Together with over sixty poets from Northern Ireland, I have included in this collection about ten or so from Britain, the United States and the Republic. In the main this has been because of their Ulster involvements and connections, but also in one or two cases simply because they have been moved to write about the present day violence. Of this group of poets I could have included many more.

The structure of the anthology is symphonic in form: the first movement serves as a prologue and contains poems which set the scene, starting off with the prehistoric days of the Bog People, and moving on to modern times, darkened with the fear that gripped the province during the Second World War and ending on a note of sudden panic after the 1969 upheaval came to a head.

The second movement centres on Derry and the smouldering fears which ultimately exploded into hatred and killing.

The third movement is the climactic section: the terror and horror of Belfast. Here the poetry is pervaded by the endless bombings, the sectarian bullets, the torture, murders, beatings and maimings.

The fourth movement contains poems dealing with the bitterness stemming from the results of violence: intimidation, frustration, the mass exodus of so many from the province, and the depression of those left behind.

I am aware that, in compiling this anthology, I might be accused of a cynical exploitation of what is, hopefully, a transient situation. It is self-evident, however, that the violence, division and hatred that, in their present acute phase, disfigure the face of Ireland have roots that go deeper and spread wider than the events of the past six years. Whether or not any of the poems in this anthology have the mark of greatness is for a future generation of readers to judge. But there is a time to keep silence and a time to speak; at the very least there is nothing in this anthology that did not cry out to be said, and that is surely more than enough to justify its existence.

Padraic Fiacc
Belfast, 1974

First Movement: Prologues

The Whin Bush

Silk of the Kine?
Sorrowful Cathleen?
Little Old Woman away in the West?
You are not these, my country.
You are a whin bush,
indestructible,
bearing all weathers,
advancing insidiously
to claim the whole field
with a flare of orange,
a thrust of green
which stabs the thieving hand.
But - how sharp that scent,
how fierce the life which bursts
out of the gnarled root,
O whin bush wild in the green field.

META MAYNE REID

On the Grand Canal: Thinking of the 'Two Nations'

Leaning forward I watch how the
dark trees, the blossom-loaded hedges,
the stiff grasses, the bent grasses, and
their exact reflections, fall behind,
while the clouds, a full tone darker
in their translation to water, run on ahead.

I look up to observe, someway in front,
a hump-backed bridge arch over and contain
in an oval, a neat landscape of small hills
which presents no originality
in its naive, obvious composition.

Black and white cattle you could see anywhere,
graze in adjacent fields
or along the tow-path.

The only unusual feature
is that an occasional cottage
shows the hipped, round thatch
which was traditional on this side
of the Black Pig's Dyke.

JOHN HEWITT

Breaking
for Will

1

The people
of the seal understand the hair-line
between
life and death. The loadstone of their

universe.
is cold. Only the snow exists,
fractured,
remaining through the breaking of

tribes and
the migration of the reindeer.

2

This
old woman
is sewing a new generation in,

preparing
the bindings of her shroud for burial
in the ice.
Months later, after trekking miles, they

may see
her face gleam out of the ice at their
fireside
and hear her song again on the winds.

3

The whales
are moving into deep southern waters,
taking
their ambergris and warm blood back.

The
old wounds sting with the change.
Alone
they travel the slow routes home.

          TREVOR McMAHON

The Tollund Man

I

Some day I will go to Aarhus
To see his peat-brown head,
The mild pods of his eye-lids,
His pointed skin cap.

In the flat country nearby
Where they dug him out,
His last gruel of winter seeds
Caked in his stomach,

Naked except for
The cap, noose and girdle,
I will stand a long time.
Bridegroom to the goddess,

She tightened her torc on him
And opened her fen,
Those dark juices working
Him to a saint's kept body,

Trove of the turfcutters'
Honeycombed workings.
Now his stained face
Reposes at Aarhus.

II

I could risk blasphemy,
Consecrate the cauldron bog
Our holy ground and pray
Him to make germinate

The scattered, ambushed
Flesh of labourers,
Stockinged corpses
Laid out in the farmyards,

Tell-tale skin and teeth
Flecking the sleepers
Of four young brothers, trailed
For miles along the lines.

III

Something of his sad freedom
As he rode the tumbril
Should come to me, driving,
Saying the names

Tollund, Grabaulle, Nebelgard,
Watching the pointing hands
Of country people,
Not knowing their tongue.

Out there in Jutland
In the old man-killing parishes
I will feel lost,
Unhappy and at home.
                    SEAMUS HEANEY

The Scar

There's not a chance now that I might recover
one syllable of what that sick man said,
tapping upon my great-grandmother's shutter,
and begging, I was told, a piece of bread,
for on his tainted breath there hung infection
rank from the cabins of the stricken west,
the spores from black potato-stalks, the spittle
mottled with poison in his rattling chest;
and she, who, by her nature, quickly answered,
accepted in return the famine-fever;
and that chance meeting, that brief confrontation,
conscribed me of the Irishry for ever.

Though much I cherish is outside their vision,
and much they prize I have no claim to share,
yet in that woman's death I found my nation:
the old woman aches and shows its fellow-scar.
                            JOHN HEWITT

Stele for a Northern Republican

Once again, with creased forehead
and trembling hands, my father calls
me from stifling darkness ...
Little enough I know of your struggle,
although you come to me more and more,
free of that heavy body armour
you tried to dissolve with alcohol,
a pale face straining in dream light
like a fish's belly
              upward to life.
Hesitantly, I trace your part in
the holy war to restore our country,
slipping from home to smoke
an absentee's mansion, concoct
ambushes. Games turned serious
when the cross-fire at Falban
riddled the tender of policemen,
one bleeding badly
              stretched upon
the stone flags of our kitchen,
your sisters moving in a whisper
of blood and bandages. Strange war
when the patrol scouted bales
of fodder, stray timber, tar
to prepare those sheltering walls
for reprisal's savage flames
if he should die!
              That night
you booked into a Strabane hotel.
'Locals were rarely used for jobs:
orders of the Dublin organizer,
shot afterwards, by his own side.'
A generation later, the only sign
of your parochial struggle was
when the plough rooted' rusty guns,
dull bayonets, in some rushy glen
for us to play with.
              Although again
and again, the dregs of disillusion
churned in our Northern parents' guts
to set their children's teeth on edge;
my mother hobbling to the shed
to burn the Free State uniforms
her two brothers had thrown off
(frugal, she saved the buttons):

my father, home from the boat at Cobh,
staring in pale anger at a Redmond
Commemoration stamp
              or tearing to
flitters the polite Masscard sent
by a Catholic policeman. But what if
you have no country to set before Christ,
only a broken province? No parades,
fierce medals, will mark Tyrone's re-birth,
betrayed by both South and North;
so lie still, difficult old man,
you were right to choose a Brooklyn slum
rather than a half-life in this
by-passed and dying place.

                              JOHN MONTAGUE

Once Alien Here (1942)

Once alien here my fathers built their house,
claimed, drained, and gave the land the shapes of use,
and for their urgent labour grudged no more
than shuffled pennies from the hoarded store
of well rubbed words that had left their overtones
in the ripe England of the mounded downs.

The sullen Irish limping to the hills
bore with them the enchantments and the spells
that in the clans' free days hung gay and rich
on every twig of every thorny hedge,
and gave the rain-pocked stone a meaning past
the blurred engraving of the fibrous frost.

So I, because of all the buried men
in Ulster clay, because of rock and glen
and mist and cloud and quality of air
as native in my thought as any here,
who now would seek a native mode to tell
our stubborn wisdom individual,
yet lacking skill in either scale of song,
the graver English, lyric Irish tongue,
must let this rich earth so enhance the blood
with steady pulse where now is plunging mood
till thought and image may, identified,
find easy voice to utter each aright.

                                JOHN HEWITT

An Ulster Prophecy

I saw the Pope breaking stones on Friday,
A blind parson sewing a patchwork quilt,
Two bishops cutting rushes with their croziers,
Roaring Meg firing rosary beads for cannonballs,
Corks in boats afloat on the summit of the Sperrins,
A severed head speaking with a grafted tongue,
A snail paring Royal Avenue with a hatchet,
British troops firing on the Shankill,
A mill and a forge on the back of a cuckoo,
The fox sitting conceitedly at a window chewing tobacco,
And a curlew in flight
              surveying
                      a United Ireland.

JOHN MONTAGUE

Visit to a School

A long narrow room with four blue
Statues of the Virgin: and silence
And schoolboys of another faith and tradition
Sit at desks, with solemn faces,
And I, expressionless, stare at each,
Conscious of the bond and break between us.

The atmosphere of this school is strange:
And strange the soft speech of the smiling
Brothers in black sashes and swaying skirts,
Who greet me each morning and afternoon:
And strange the shy, sidelong glances
Of these children, harsh in speech,
Who playing handball, halt courteously
And smile as I pass them by.
And everyone is kind; yet I feel the strangeness.
Even the names on this dull roll-book
Have a strange music: Dominic and Finbarra;
Columba and Hilary, Silvester and Malachi,
Laurence and Gerard. And I glance
At each child as I call his name;
And their tired faces recall my own childhood
In this same city, but a different childhood.
And all this week, morning and afternoon
We have met, these children and I,
With hardly a dozen words spoken

Between us: but I know their faces, they mine,
And we smile in the playground, or meeting
Casually in the street nod greeting.

And now this week of June,
Is ended; and now I've left this school
Of pale children with strange names,
Children who may see some harmony
In this place I call native;
But I am conscious of the bond and break
Between us.

JOHN BOYD

The Dilemma (1969)

Born in this island, maimed by history
and creed-infected, by my father taught
the stubborn habit of unfettered thought
I dreamed, like him, all people should be free,
So, while my logic steered me well outside
that ailing church which claims dominion
over the questing spirit, I denied
all credence to the state by rebels won
from a torn nation, rigged to guard their gain,
though they assert their love of liberty,
which craft has narrowed to a fear of Rome,
So, since this ruptured country is my home,
it long has been my bitter luck to be
caught in the cross-fire of their false campaign.

JOHN HEWITT

from Prolegomena
for John Smith

But here the idiom's Lowland Scots
Not Gaelic-biting, scouring
As caustic soda; spiky as whin
Guarding its ground against encroachment;
Bitter as nicotine, chewed plug
Squirted from the corner of the mouth.
It scalds the ear, red-hot steel
Plunged hissing into water.
You handle it with pincers, bang

The rivets home, every stroke
A wince and jar from wrist and brain.

NORMAN DUGDALE

An Ulsterman in England Remembers

Here at a distance, rocked by hopes and fears
with each convulsion of that fevered state,
the chafing thoughts attract, in sudden spate,
neglected shadows from my boyhood years:
the Crossley tenders caged and roofed with wire,
the crouching Black and Tans, the Lewis gun,
the dead lad in the entry; one by one
the Catholic public-houses set on fire;
the anxious curfew of the summer night
the thoroughfares deserted, at a door
three figures standing, till the tender's roar,
approaching closer, drives them out of sight;
and on the broad roof of the County Gaol
the singing prisoners brief freedom take
to keep an angry neighbourhood awake
with rattled plate and pot and metal pail;
below my bedroom-window, bullet-spark
along the kerb, the beat of rapid feet
of the lone sniper, clipping up the street,
soon lost, the gas-lamps shattered, in the dark;
and on the paved edge of our cinder-field,
intent till dusk upon the game, I ran
against a briskly-striding, tall young man,
and glimpsed the rifle he thought well-concealed.
At Auschwitz, Dallas, I felt no surprise
when violence across the world's wide screen,
declared the age imperilled; I had seen
the future in that frightened gunman's eyes.

JOHN HEWITT

The Reina Del Mar

I know the cobwebbed squint
She casts at foreign colour on the cheek,
How she snuffles at vagrancy.
Cocks a sow's ear to accents.
I know to creep in and out

Of this place
While the mislocated sun
Drums on the irritating patchwork
Of her quilt,
Her bedlumps;
While the concupiscent flies
Lull about the hot manure,
And the peninsula stretches
Like a long, elastic snore
Into the Irish Sea.

              GEORGE McWHIRTER

Ballykinlar: May 1940

One standing on the empty beach
beyond the sandhills, threw wide his arms
with an oratorical gesture to beseech
the blue and unresponsive hills:

> let now Cuchulain or some of the old gods
> descend from the mountains, with chariot wheels
> scything the hordes of evil, wielding again
> the battle-axe for justice, before all else fails.

And yet, the Red Branch withered at the last
now only a shadow in the mind of man
the victors and the victims - they are all lost
and the shed blood forgotten.
                   Not out of the hills
must come the conquering host, but from the deep
recesses of the heart before the darkness falls.

              PATRICK MAYBIN

Under Orion

Orion marching westward still
Night over all
And on the lion shores
Of ancient Albion an uneasy tide
Scarcely rising or falling
Bides oily and sluggish
As wakeful among the sleeping millions
I wonder do they yet know where they are going

Or is it not true they have lost their way
Whose fathers held the turning world in fee?

I only know I have seen Mangan's ghost
Heard long since his last departing moan
And across the Irish sea
Ulster's Red Hand uplifted
Salutes those about to die
Oh there will be blood, be vengeance
The raven will tear with his bitter beak
At Cuchulain's side
And blood's redundance overflow the Erne
       in spate indeed

But Maeve and her three-pronged staff
       shall not prevail
Though Ulster's wound unstaunched
       bleeds white the world
Cuchulain tied to his rock will hold the pass
And yet, and yet
It was not now but long ago I heard that ghost
Most haggard moan he had been wrecked
       on beauty's shore
But who in those far-off days had paid me any mind
I was a young poet then who now am old am blind
And it may be that grief for the dying and the dead
Muffles the warning note that I would sound.

                            EWART MILNE

Street Names

I hear the street names on the radio
and map reported bomb or barricade:
this was my childhood's precinct, and I know
how such streets look, down to the very shade
of brick, of paintwork on each door and sill,
what school or church nearby one might attend,
if there's a chance to glimpse familiar hill
between the chimneys where the grey slates end.

Yet I speak only of appearances,
a stage unpeopled, not the tragic play:
though actual faces of known families

flash back across the gap of fifty years;
can these be theirs, the children that today
rage in the fetters of their fathers' fears?

JOHN HEWITT

Nightmare

In this dream I am carrying a pig,
Cradling in my arms its deceptive grin,
The comfortable folds of its baby limbs,
The feet coyly disposed like a spaniels.

I am in charge of its delivery,
Taking it somewhere, and feeling oddly
And indissolubly attached to it -
There is nothing I can do about it,

Not even when it bites into my skull
Quite painlessly, and eats my face away,
Its juices corroding my memory,
The chamber of straight lines and purposes,

Until I am carrying everywhere
Always, on a dwindling zig-zag, the pig.

MICHAEL LONGLEY

Black Cat

When it gets darker
any room is familiar,

You see things clearer
like a cat.

Presence is just a body
bare like breath,

the window
no one's going to jump from,
the chair
safe as a house.

But there is always more,

something awkward
to get used to:

the place where a kid
says, my coat's a bomb,
where a man walks
with a coffin, terrified and dumb.

Part squeals, Let me out,
but the cat stays the same.

It points the finger.
It knows how to blame.

GERALD DAWE

A Belfastman Abroad Argues with Himself

Admit the fact, you might have stood your ground
and kept one corner clear for decency,
making no claims, but like a friendly tree,
offering shade to those who'd gather round.
You should have spoken when that evil man
first raised his raucous shout, to all who lied
given the lie direct, that little clan
who later marched for justice, joined with pride.

Now from safe distance, you assert your right
to public rage. This town is, after all,
where I was born and lived for fifty years.
I knew its crooked masters well by sight,
endured its venom and survived its sneers -
I scratch these verses on its flame-scorcht wall.

JOHN HEWITT

New Year's Eve 1969

Ring out the old, ring in the new.
What's changed? The ghosts of '98,
Fitzgerald, Emmet and Wolfe Tone,
Who set the pitchforks at the cannon
To rip the rotten fabric down,
Stalk across our midnight yet.
They thought the brotherhood of man

Would spring from jobbers, placemen, crooks,
The desperate and destitute.
Why should they fret, who constellate
In one eclectic pantheon
As founding fathers of the state
With all those whom the self-same dream
Drugged? – each philosophic simpleton
By Yeats' rhetoric magnified
With silly women like Maude Gonne
MacBride and Constance Markievicz.
But Castlereagh addressed with strict
Compassion to his craft, cold eye
Disdaining cant, who knew the cry
Must end in blood, the frenzy pitch
All in confusion of the ditch,
Guilt, innocence alike be flung
Torn and spitted on the dung
For pigs to root in; he who whipped
The pack to heel on either side
Slavering for its kill; then blew
His brains out at the afterdate -
God knows from what despair or grief -
Earned his ironic epitaph:
The patriot died execrate.

                             NORMAN DUGDALE

Night-Ferry

Winking headlands dowsed by dawn
Smudge to shore on either bow. The Lough
Wrinkles, swells, a slow fat slug
Mounting Belfast's languid loin

Slobbing rocks from which gulls rise
To drift astern. Like rusty tramps
Mills and wharves slide broadside on,
Dribbling slops from their stained sides.

Confetti strews the puddled quay
Where wedding-parties roared farewell
The night before or sobbed through veils
To watch the stern-lights fade. Beyond

Wall-slogans run like wet mascara
Down gable-ends. The terraces

Wear jilted looks, deserted
In the morning, swollen-eyed,

But last night's rain has rinsed the streets
Of last night's vomit, last night's blood,
'Where to, sir?' asks the taximan. 'Home,'
I say. 'Where's that?' 'Home's here,' I say, 'for good.'

NORMAN DUGDALE

Cage Under Siege

This is home. This is the Irish North.
Where we endure the earth's falling away
Rivets an iron sky to north and west.
Where the covetous South darkens, granite
Rears a grave wall. Eastward the sea recoils
Toward England, breathless with horror, sobs back.

On our borders the known world ends sheer.
We've pulled the sea around us like a shawl
And heaved the mountains higher. The waiting
South's bog-barbarians starve against a grand
Squiggle on our map. The sky is closed.
This is home. This is the Irish North.

PATRICK WILLIAMS

Glengormley

Wonders are many and none is more wonderful than man
Who has tamed the terrier, trimmed the hedge
And grasped the principle of the watering can.
Clothes-pegs litter the window-ledge
And the long ships lie in clover. Washing lines
Shake out white linen over the chalk thanes.

Now we are safe from monsters, and the giants
Who tore up sods twelve miles by six
And hurled them out to sea to become islands
Can worry us no more. The sticks
And stones that once broke bones will not now harm
A generation of such sense and charm.

Only words hurt us now. No saint or hero,
Landing at night from the conspiring seas,
Brings dangerous tokens to the new era -
Their sad names linger in the histories.
The unreconciled, in their metaphysical pain,
Strangle on lamp-posts in the dawn rain

And much dies with them. I should rather praise
A wordly time under this worldly sky -
The terrier-taming, garden-watering days
Those heroes pictured as they struggled through
The quick noose of their finite being. By
Necessity, if not choice, I live here too.

DEREK MAHON

Death in the Glen
Collin Glen 1968

Known for your sausages,
Screaming pigs,
And the dry decay of
Ashes from the burnhouse;

Once you were beautiful,
As the leaves flickered,
Light and shade,
As the young trout leaped
And plopped,
And as the cool clear water
Cascaded down the hillside;

Now the slime vomits
Over the rocks,
The green death creeps
Through the glen,
And the ashes settle,
soak,
and submerge in the water.

MICHAEL BROPHY

Against Oncoming Civil War
for Brendan Hamill

Salmon silvering grey to die
What summers of the past day

Trapped in our own shallow chill
Shadows, then slowly, a whole season's
Twilight, bleeds like a blue-blood's at
The least scathing, opens out

The silk cloud's spider-fingering pine
Against (Is it any wonder?)
The running away from us - sky

Cannot be wrenched back nor hoarded
But given only as the black ever -
greens go on giving high up over
The mountain hill high up over
This little mill town, the mornings
Getting darker than sun down.

      PADRAIC FIACC

The Iron Circle
to the memory of the late W R Rodgers

Here, often, a man provoked has said his say,
stung by opinion or unjust event,
and found his angry words, to his dismay,
prop up his adversary's argument,
for bitterness is not allowed to die,
is fanned and fuelled, in this crazy land:
the brandished gun demands a gun's reply;
hate answers hate, our crest the Bloody Hand.

My friend, who followed coursing on this ground,
and sought its lore and logic everywhere,
suggested once, the Hare must need the Hound
as surely as the Hound must need the Hare.
In my mood now I fear that he was right:
the chase continues, with no end in sight.

      JOHN HEWITT

Daisymount Terrace
3 January, 1974

1

From the school in the Church Quarter
Lately laden with books and tasks
My brother whooped downhill
Fighting allcomers, back
To paraffin lamps and griddle bread
The Moat and the Church overhead,
And the Reverend Cottar poised
Pruning his sermon, but
The stream behind the houses stole
Pebbling his sleep:

For Daisymount Terrace
Was beyond the tramlines
And the festering city's war
And himself with his popgun lost
Between the opposing armies -
But the stream had no name
Peopling his sleep serene
Among humpedup fields

And the cottages
Gape Row limewashed, the gardens
Stammering up to the Moat:
And old bent kitchen spoons
Digging for giants' bones;
Dundonald a breath between
Beechfield Street eviction -
GET OUT OR BE BURNED OUT -
And later the house with the garden
Welcomed and planted and groomed
By certain familiar hands
Of our father creating our world.

2

Gardening I look at my hands
Veined like his the stream
Still stumbling unnamed
And myself also aghast
Between the opposing armies -
Slow to pluck weeds -
For Daisymount Terrace now
Lacks fields for a daisychain
For a mayor in a frightened town.

The stream stumbles unnamed
And a tithe
Of the Church Quarter
Enfolds the school while I
Stumble downhill lacking
A shout from my brother
His keeper and sleeper
His brother grown in his place
With a father's hands and stance
In forgotten remembered ground.

3

With nettles in my hands
In an innocent afternoon
My brother running back
With whose guilt in my hands
The stream a gutter now
Silenced by traffic ground
To a redhanded stop
A rumour of bombs -
I listen hand at ear
For a mercy of water and
My brother's confident shout
In an innocent afternoon.

      ROY McFADDEN

Autumn 1939

McFadden hawked 'Peace News' in Royal Avenue,
Outraged the moon-faced citizens.
END THE WAR! PEACE NOW!

While I was buying stamps in the GPO
For frantic letters to Irene.
END THE WAR! PEACE NOW!

McFadden showed me his singing poems.
I said: 'John Keats is dead.'
END THE WAR! PEACE NOW!

Leaves choked the Stranmillis gutters,
Slow fuses smouldered up the Falls.
END THE WAR! PEACE NOW!
      ROBERT GREACEN

The Glorious Twelfth
(12 July, 1943)

You will remember that the Twelfth was always dry,
That rain followed the day after, some said as Judgement,
While others argued that drums of Ulster stirring
Pulled out the corded wetness from our local skies.
Four years ago we heard them last, heard the thunder
Smouldering through the ribboned streets towards the battle
In the fields of Finaghy. There was fire then,
Fire in our throats, fire beaten out from our cities,
Cold, distant, strongly arid in the normal weather:
Four years ago since last we heard the drums' thunder,
Since the Orange banners looped in gay procession
And bands of lute and fife, or brass and silver
Played hell to the Pope and immortality to William -
To William, Prince of Orange, defender and avenger,
To William, the stiff Dutch Protestant, who saved us
From villainous James, the tyrant Stuart King.

Remember 1690, remember the ancient wrongs of Rome
Remember Derry, Aughrim, Enniskillen and the Boyne,
The glorious Boyne in Ireland, where the Pope was overcome,
Remember the Maiden City and the breaking of her boom.

These were my people marching on the streets,
Released from inhibition and resolved to keep the faith.
Four years since fire has run swift rivers into Europe
From Dunkirk to Briansk, from Naples to Novgorod,
From Caucasus to Clyde, from Warsaw to Belfast.
And now, in Derry and Downpatrick no Ulstermen are marching
To the rustle of their banners and the flogging of their drums.
Our red-brick cities have their blackened skeletons,
Our people carry the public and the personal wound.

Forgotten 1690, forgotten the ancient wrongs of Rome,
Forgotten Derry, Aughrim, Enniskillen and the Boyne,
The glorious Boyne in Ireland where the Pope was overcome,
Forgotten the Maiden City and the breaking of her boom.

You will remember that the Twelfth was always dry,
While now in Italy the bloods of Continents are joined,
While now the Russian plains are stacked with corpses,
Rotting in the Red sun, feeding plagues to common rats ...
But after carnage there will be music; after death will be hope,
After the horror of the day will come the evening dream,
After hatred's harvest joy will march, shrouded, to Finaghy.

ROBERT GREACEN

Coup de Grace 1973

The Military are tearing down
What is left of the burnt out

House; (nothing for it but that
It spits bricks and mortar now ...)

The derrick is swinging a stone ball
Demolishes the foundation. The bull-

dozer's teeth are deep set in the coal
Hole where we hid from the spring
Sky of forty-one, and if you

Were an 'oul Teigue', clutched
        a 'houl' of
The Infant of Prague, and cursed
        and prayed
'Hell to my soule' the night the ground shook
A good thirty two years ago!

(Today my 'good-living' neighbours
Finish off the Huns' dirty-work.)

                        PADRAIC FIACC

Letter to Derek Mahon

And did we come into our own
When, minus muse and lexicon,
We traced in August sixty-nine
Our imaginary Peace Line
Around the burnt-out houses of
The Catholics we'd scarcely loved,
Two Sisyphuses come to budge
The sticks and stones of an old grudge.

Two poetic conservatives
In the city of guns and long knives;
Our ears receiving then and there
The stereophonic nightmare
Of the Shankill and the Falls,
Our matches struck on crumbling walls
To light us as we moved at last
Through the back alleys of Belfast?

Why it mattered to have you here
You who journeyed to Inishere
With me, years back, one Easter when
With MacIntyre and the lone Dane
Our footsteps lifted up the larks,
Echoing off those western rocks
And down that darkening arcade
Hung with the failures of our trade,

Will understand. We were tongue-tied
Companions of the island's dead
In the graveyard among the dunes,
Eavesdroppers on conversations
With a Jesus who spoke Irish -
We were strangers in that parish,
Black tea with bacon and cabbage
For our sacraments and pottage.

Dank blankets making up our tent
Till, islanders ourselves, we bent
Our knees and cut the watery sod
From the lazy-bed where slept a God
We couldn't count among our friends,
Although we'd taken in our hands
Splinters of driftwood nailed and stuck
On the rim of the Atlantic.

That was Good Friday years ago -
How persistent the undertow
Slapped by currachs ferrying stones,
Moonlight glossing the confusions
Of its each bilingual wave - yes,
We would have lingered there for less ...
Six islanders for a ten bob note
Rowed us out to the anchored boat.

                    MICHAEL LONGLEY

Testament
for Marie

I remember the dour walls
names on plaques
of men gone down
at Somme and Lyons,
the noisy tiles

the congregation flocked on
eyed by Rector
plain-singing man,
the guide and mentor
of thrill and thrift,
squat, heavy-jawed
smelling like a dentist,
unritualising clerk
and apprentice:
No fire and brimstone
or Holy Ghost,
I chopped and changed,
undamaged,
         cursed
for New Year Mass
backed by porter
and a keen Catholic lass
entered unhallowed
the sanctimonious,
devil-scared by the dark
head-bowed mass,
bleary-eyed, chanting
blackness,
         the rise
and fall - one voice
raised above them all;
candle, altar, robe,
awesoming penitent
unused to sacrament
communed like this.
The nailed effigy
high above the nave,
no more naive
to testament.

         GERALD DAWE

Poem in Belfast
for Michael Longley

Walking among my own this windy morning
In a tide of sunlight between shower and shower,
I resume my old conspiracy with the wet
Stone and the unwieldy images of the squinting heart.
Once more, as before, I remember not to forget.

There is a perverse pride in being on the side
Of the fallen angels, and refusing to get up.
We could all be saved by keeping an eye on the hill
At the top of every street, for there it is -
Eternally, if irrelevantly, visible -

But yield instead to the humourous formulae.
The phoney mystery in the knowing nod.
We keep our sullen silence in light and shade,
Rehearsing our astute salvations under
The cold gaze of a sanctimonious God.

One part of my mind must learn to know its place -
The things that happen in the kitchen-houses
And echoing back-streets of this desperate city
Should engage more than my transient interest,
Exact more interest than my casual pity.

DEREK MAHON

Where Are My People Now?

Reared in the iron rods
Of the Northern rain,
And the grey dour dust
Of the Protestant city;

But brought up with
The half suppressed yearnings
Of the Catholic Falls Road,
To the children's stories
Of Pearse and of Connolly,
Dan Breen and Sean Tracy
And the Black and Tan raids
On the Duffins and McMahons;

But then State educated,
Carefully creamed off,
Cultivated by Stormont
Until now in the suburbs,
With my Methodist neighbours,
My mortgage and
Oath of Allegiance job;

I sit in my neat new
Government subsidy, semi detached
And watch the riot squad
Baton charge down the Falls;

See my friends and relations
With black blood on their faces
And their cracked open skulls;

Now, I taste my own blood,
And feel the old fear,
And see the iron bar
Smash into his nose;

But it's the Falls Road
That is fighting,
Not this New Ulster Image,
The thin layer of veneer
Slides and seals over;

Where is my life?
Who are my people, Now?

MICHAEL BROPHY

Heritages
for Ethel

Would have taken
you years
for this
to detail
warped visions
in my head
of the ground
feeding City
& black sky

in this chapel
built with the hand
of Eighty Five Pounds from
'Belfast Volunteers'
out to prove their
18th century liberal-
mindedness

(a kind of
dream machine threshing
fragments)

from when
granny came in
to take the weight

off her feet
& hope to God
whatever it was
would turn out right.

I blubber
before votive
candlelight
knowing only
half-measures
inside & out

'blood-
    sacrifice' rage
from pavements,
        ghosts
its way
through terror
to spiritual
condolence ...

get right
all pious gestures
inside & out
where a soldier
died from
crackshot at
blankrange

... looking like
death warmed up
at the sight
of skin scorched yellow
listening to
small doors snib shut
conspiracies of
silence whispered at
handrails. All
read my blind-
drunk signs.
        I head
out to the street
world with
wonder wobbling
where tears jerked
for this
        I was born.

        GERALD DAWE

Nan

It was an ease for her to die they said
Platitude of consolation,
How could they know how hard she tried
To die outside the Union walls.
Her life was lived in short back lanes,
Between that Union and two jails,
But there was strength of hope in her would shame
The affected posing fools
Who mock the mystery of love.

True enough her schooling ended in third book,
And she could sing
The Towns and petty mills of Monaghan,
In proof of it.

But when she took her man dying to her bed,
Though others would not touch the cups he used,
She had a love that is not learned
By piping quirks about some others' books.
And if life left her lingeringly,
And with the raw bed rash of years,
Those wordless days and restless nights,
that drifted into one sewer-smelling haze
Were not a hopeless waiting for release in death,
But a purgatory on earth she always hoped
Would end before she left.

And had a car once, in the twenties,
And through the next debt-racked decades,
She kept a faded photograph of it,
And felt she would again
Lift up her head in that backbiting town,
And prove herself in front of them.
Her man was popular, but a rogue,
And lost too many jobs to be believed
By any but her,
Who, while others growled or frowned,
Or sneering cut in public places,
Never once put blame of this or that on him,
But bent - with him she thought -
To some new ploy to keep the Sheriff out.
But while she strained her failing frame
He played the local matches once again
Through many taverns in the tattling town.

But when he died there was much more
Than that old and battered car of forty years before:
For hours he roared as cancer
Tore the soul from his taut and spindly bones,
And tossed in throes of lonely agony until
They sent for her.
Her buckling knees drove rusty wheels,
The long road to the hospital.
Quiet tears gripped her throat and she
The book she daily prayed at Mass;
Her tears for him turned back his years

And lifted now the fears of pain,
And when her swollen hand came dripping wet
From brows that had no school for this
He smiled and spoke.
And smiled at ease the while she knelt
And prayed with him, and stayed with him
To see him smiling, praying at the end.

And when the house came down
It was not because of Sheriff or of debt,
But since some civil servant had decreed,
New roads in place of lanes.

Her proof was not to men
Who saw the coffin built of institution deal,
But to the God she met each day at Mass,
Until her legs no longer moved
And then,
He came at seven, as she by habit tried to rise.

OLIVER SNODDY

Elegy in 'The Holy Land'
for Sean Breslin

Girl with the whooping cough
           gliding
Through the wall-tall, caved-in
Cliffs of us being kids
           (still building
'Dragon Teeth Barricades')

Hankering after the way, you, rosey
With ear aches
           hung limp over

Fire-bombed iron now, I
Cannot think how long ago

It was your small unsmiling
        self
With a doll's pram, scraping
           down through
A childhood still in hell for boys
Who tease
        echoing out of sheep-
ishness our wolf
           'Hello-Good-byes'

Forget your name even
      in
         this
Black shame on us low-
land Scotch drunks call being alive

O dolly-Eurydice, my dark Ros-
aleen dream
        of bog on bog of bone-
grounded cloud, Ireland, my dear

Dragon seed pod ...

                PADRAIC FIACC

Meditations on the Suspension of Stormont 1972
Crete 1972

I

For my mother I would build a monument
if I were skilled in masonry, a tower
of Carrick stone to guard her
from the raven's flight.
A lace-maker, she could stitch
pictures of innocence out of this night's drunkenness,
protected from the call of madmen dressed in madmen's masks,
battering on the wall.

But being poor, and having only words,
rough words at that, the words of farmers,
can I make a thing so fine
that she would hang it on her wall?

Can I hope from truth to fall
into the heart of beauty? A word, that's all,
the unscabbard word, a word to end all words,
my father shouts, 'To end it all! A war!
To end all words!' The raven's call;

Have done with dreaming.

II

My father when he was
a proud and handsome man -
his hands could easily encircle
my mother's waist when they were dancing -
gave me land, six counties
that he said I owned: 'This land,' he said,
'Is our heart's land.
Your uncle fought for it in Germany,
Your cousin died for it in Egypt.
Everywhere the word, the promised flesh
was Ulster's. It is your birthright and the wing
which will protect you, always.

For over there is neighbour's land,
and mother's uncle is a rector in Fermanagh.
A man I went to school with
owns the heart of Antrim.
It is our heart's land.
And it was given

by an act of Parliament.'

III

Heath and Maudling break their word,
to promised flesh they break their pledge,
and the battle-fields in Europe vomit up their groaning dead
to witness this fresh sacrilege.

A myth becomes reality,
and so a song begins

Eight hundred men
brought Stormont down
Now proddie is confusion's clown ...

the masks go on; the dance begins;

all now are gathered in that black myth's wing -
as if a word from me could have changed anything.

IV

My mother in the weeping room
of our small house in Belfast
stitches out a final landscape,
of how we lived, how once we lived,
long walks at dusk, the harvest bells,
church on Sunday and the country school,
tales to tell
of sailors and the grey sea.
Of saints and servants,
stories in the hall.

At last she looks upon our final landscape,
but now sees blood where she had stitched the sky:
she cries out once, 'Have done with dreaming,
all my pictures tell a lie!'

The rebels come,
they burn her pictures, break her loom.
And soldiers, turning, find her
weeping
in her weeping room.

                                        SHAUN TRAYNOR

At 69 Alliance Road, Belfast: 1967

i

In the brow sweat of racked flesh
my mother battled with the vicious
crab, on her feet and in bed,
and when the cropped leaf fell to earth,
she died, her body derelict
that on the earth had multiplied.

ii

The concrete coping cracked
at the seams and separate
on top; the bricks weathered,
broken and suddenly
old after my absence.
Paint brushed unusually
on to the rim of the glass
of this window where I watch
and brood. My father's hands

are old and weathered building ships
in the cut of the wind on the sea's edge
to feed more mouths than his own
and when love is living under the same
roof. Each paint supersedes
the former until someone
someday will scrape back
and start anew in this house.

iii

My father worked in the shipyard,
was never maimed by book or word
to do otherwise. He hoofed it
up the back road to where the distant
buses, like lanterns, turned at Ardoyne.
He loved the walk to warm himself.
His feet rapped on the road round the side
of the house through the morning darkness.
He always walked on the road. He said,
the pavement flags would only break
his neck. My mother sometimes came
back to bed for an hour.
                With an
uncle he scrapped in booths for sport
and the same evening starred in
dancing pumps and pomade. They trained
greyhounds in the country and between
them at one sitting ate a stone
of spuds and couldn't budge for a while.
The dogs were fast and properly fed.
His brother, years dead now,
left Ireland and fought a war
in an American uniform.
My father plugged his days of wind
and rain-damp clothes in the rusted steel
guts of ships, his bone joints swollen and locked.
Forty years of ships he has seen
sail down Belfast Lough and regrets
in his spited bone the bare years.

iv

'Chop sticks on Sunday,'
my mother said,
'and be the moon's sad
cameo.' She never read
but loved word and song.

I renegued my father's tools
and my mother's church,
left my dungarees empty
on the peg in their house
and sailed out of Ireland
six years ago. Now I return.
My mother is in her coffin.
The quiet well of her ingrown
wisdom and love where I bucketed
for twenty years is closed.
I have learned her identity
in myself. I plumb the moving stream
for the hard integer stones,
white on the bottom, worked
round by the water's whirl.

     JOHNSTON KIRKPATRICK

The Forge

My grandfather was a blacksmith,
A small man with a battered hat
And a grey scrubbing brush moustache.
His forge was on a mountain
Wooden, rotted, green with moss,
And when the salt spray
Curdled over from Omeath
Even the black gleam of the anvil
Faded and tarnished,
Until the forge became
Only a children's plaything,
Hooped barrels of slime
Clotted with dead wasps,
And hammers, tongs and trollies
Ash grey with dust,
Netted with black cobwebs.

Until today,
When a strange Patrick
Returns to his Slemish,
To the small fields
Stitched with bald boulders
Brown with dead bracken,
To the mist wet wastes
Of Annavernagh,

Where now
Only the blank black
Faces of the sheep
Are staring from the stones.

        MICHAEL BROPHY

Big Ned

'A real horse of a man,' McTaggart
Called him, 'Nineteen hands high
With shoulders like a barn-door.'
Townland's champion, miser and horsedoctor,
Focus of all the neighbours' shallow gossip,
Uncle Eddy strode Brockagh's rushy acres,
Alone for eighty years, to outlive them all.
Unschooled and illiterate, a product of
Lean times, (he bought his first suit
With rabbits snared from the Lough shore)
He could guide a team of Clydesdales at ten,
At fifteen a man.

Rebuffed, a sullen parish admired his
Feats from a safe distance -
Fearing the hard honesty, the cold stare;
When he mowed all night in the 'Wet Meadow',
Lifted a trap across his bare shoulders,
Broke stallions, or drove a herd of
Bullocks to the Moy Fair, alone.
Well-able for pestering clergy, friendless
And woman-less all his life, he christened the
Great Bays 'Jack' and 'Jim' caring only that the
Lame collie 'Watch' shared his
Turf-piled hearth, in the long winter nights.

'Laid out three police,' McTaggart marvelled,
'At Finnegan's Republican funeral.'
Finally, as lawyers and clergy prepared
To divide his money
The whole parish waited triumphantly for the
Last feat, when alone as ever, at the end,
He chased doctor and priest from his death-bed,
Wanting only the work-man
To bring the horses to the window,
So that he could see them.

        TOM McGURK

The Brethren

Arraigned by silence, I recall
The noise of lecture-rooms,
School refectories and dining hall,
A hundred faces in a hundred spoons,
Raised in laughter or in prayer bent,
Each distorted and each innocent.

Torrential sunshine falling through the slate
Made marquetries of light upon the floor.
I still recall those greasy Belfast flats
Where parties hit upon a steady roar
Of subdued violence and lent
Fury to the Sabbaths which we spent

Hung over empty streets where Jimmy Witherspoon
Sang under the needle old laments
Of careless love and shivered moon,
Evoked the whorish armpit scents
Of Negro brothels while the Plymouth Brethren
Two doors down sat sunk in heaven.

Stupor Sunday, stupor mundi. What was to come
If not the eyes that were growing
Above violent mouths in the light-in-dark aquarium
Of the Sunday's splashless, deep-sown
Peace? What if it were shattered?

Recently I found old photographs
Fallen behind the attic water-tank,
And saw my friends were now the staffs
Of great bureaucracies. Some frames stank
Of mildew, some were so defaced
That half the time I couldn't put a face

On half of them. Some were dead.
The water had seeped through a broken housing
Had slowly savaged all those eyes and heads.
I felt its closing coldness dousing
Those black American and white hummed tunes,
The faces echoed in those hammered spoons.

              SEAMUS DEANE

The Maze

We glint like metal fish
Trapped beneath a sieve of light,
Scales and fins moulded in one die.
Custodians of silver and of gold,
Believe the noble lie:

When you made my hands, you shaped
Them with barbed wire. The flesh
Congealed beneath the twisted net -
Head-line, heart-line, fate-line,
The eradicable scars.

CIARAN CARSON

Outside Looking In

Miles of high-wire fencing
thousands of arc lights
protect us from him.

At 21, already a father
his kind is dangerous.

An intellectual with a brain of his own
a stubborn sod who won't conform.

He must be broken
forced to worship the beast,
the system,
the war-machine
with its bloody rag of history.

Inside
caged solitudes
betrayal and rejection,
measure his manhood less each day.

While outside
we, skilled in the language of living,
make only rude noises
as always,
happy to be on the outside
looking in.

GERALD McFLYNN

Internee

It is not absolutely fair.
It is not absolutely wrong
And it does not hurt
To be jeered at
When you are hanging
Upside down
When hanging upside down hurts more.

The far-off neons of Belfast glint like crosses.
I'm lying in blood, piss, pus, slime.
My face is at the feet of the Supreme
Victim, the people, the people who
Are utterly lost.

I grope but all I can do
Is open my fists wide and
Shoot them back tight in again.

The social worker, the part-time
Student teacher and/or
University lecturer
Volunteer to help
Fob me off with words
As the prison GP with aspros
But how can *they* tell where it hurts?

My left ball, my right ball,
My belly hole, my arse hole?

I'm in here for just being

Fixed like the crucified, writhing,
Not able to rest, immobile, yet
Sucked down yet yanked back up
To where ever you are

Thrown down born alive.

                         PADRAIC FIACC

Whatever you say, say nothing

1

I'm writing just after an encounter
with an English journalist in search of 'views
on the Irish thing'. I'm back in winter
quarters where bad news is no longer news,

where media men are stringers, sniff and point
where zoom lenses and uhers and coiled leads
litter the hotels. The times are out of joint
but I incline as much to rosary beads

as to the jottings and analyses
of leader-writers or newspapermen
who've scribbled down the long campaign from gas
and protest to gelignite and sten,

who proved upon their pulses 'escalate',
'backlash' and 'crack down', 'the Provisional wing',
'polarisation' and 'long-standing hate',
yet I live here, I live here too, I sing

expertly civil-tongued with civil neighbours
on the high wires of first wireless reports,
sucking the false tastes, the stony flavours
of those sanctioned, old elaborate retorts:

'oh, it's disgraceful, surely, I agree,'
'Where's it going to end?' 'It's getting worse,'
'They're murderers,' 'Internment, understandably,'
The 'voice of sanity' is getting hoarse.

2

Men die at hand. In blasted street and home
the gelignite, a common sound effect;
as the man said when Celtic won, 'the Pope of Rome
's a happy man this night.' His flock suspect

in their deepest heart of hearts the heretic
has come at last to heel and to the stake.
We tremble near the flames but want no truck
with the actual firing. We're on the make

as ever. Long sucking the hind tit
cold as a witch's and as hard to swallow
still leaves us fork-tongued on the border bit:
the liberal papist note sounds hollow

when amplified and mixed in with the bangs
that shake all hearts and windows day and night.
(It's tempting here to rhyme on 'labour pangs'
and diagnose a rebirth in our plight

but that would be to ignore other symptoms.
Last night you didn't need a stethoscope
to hear the eructation of Orange drums
allergic equally to Pearse and Pope.)

On all sides 'little platoons' are mustering -
the phrase is Cruise O'Brien's via that great
backlash, Burke - while I sit here with a pestering
drouth for words at once both gaff and bait

to lure the tribal shoals to epigram
and order. I believe any of us
could draw the line through bigotry and sham
given the right line, *aere perennius*.

3

'Religion's never mentioned here,' of course.
'You know them by their eyes,' and hold your tongue.
'One side's as bad as the other,' never worse.
Christ, it's near time that some small leak was sprung

in the great dykes the Dutchman made
to dam the dangerous tide that followed Seamus.
Yet for all this art and sedentary trade
I am incapable. The famous

Northern reticence, the tight gag of place
and times: yes, yes. Of the wee six I sing
Where to be saved you only must save face
and whatever you say, you say nothing.

Smoke-signals are loud-mouthed compared with us:
manoeuvrings to find out name and school,
subtle discrimination by addresses
with hardly an exception to the rule

that Norman, Ken and Sidney signalled Prod
and Seamus (call me Sean) were sure-fire Pape.
O land of password, handgrip, wink and nod,
of open minds as open as a trap,

where tongues lie coiled, as under flames lie wicks,
where half of us, as in a wooden horse
were cabin'd and confined like wily Greeks,
besieged within the siege, whispering morse.

4

This morning from a dewy motorway
I saw the new camp for the internees:
a bomb had left a crater of fresh clay
in the roadside, and over in the trees

machine-gun posts defined a real stockade.
There was that white mist you get on a low ground
and it was *dejà-vu*, some film made
of Stalag 17, a bad dream with no sound.

Is there a life before death? That's chalked up
in Ballymurphy. Competence with pain,
coherent miseries, a bite and sup,
we hug our little destiny again.

SEAMUS HEANEY

Second Movement: Derry

Bitter Harvest

The land is banked
like a sullen fire; trees secretive
behind opaque barriers of fog; lights
a welling blur in a silver haze.
Children, fading from the streets
like sunset marigolds,
ring up the curtain on the macabre play
enacted nightly on a shattered stage.
Autumnal tapestries glow and fade
before unseeing eyes; the acrid smell
of burning leaves stings nostrils already raw
with petrol fumes; and beechwood gold
melts all too swiftly in sectarian fire.

                              ELEANOR MURRAY

Bonfire

God is too much the way he asks of me
That I understand others too,
And that, when I fail, as I do, I do,
That I pray for them as well
Instead of damning them to his hell
When he created for us too.

If you throw seawood on the fire
The flames are alive with the submarine
Greed of the salt and the cold water,
And their elemental odours wake the room
To its own violent charms.
More in light than with heat they consume

One another, God hungers for situations
That only the devil could invent.
I remember our religious festivals,
Bonfires hanging vulpine on the trees

In long flickering shadows.
And the crowds, engulfed in the burning, content.

SEAMUS DEANE

From Singing School
for Seamus Deane

Well, as Kavanagh said, we have lived
In important places. The lonely scarp
Of St Columb's College, where I billeted
For six years, overlooked your Bogside.
I gazed into new worlds: the inflamed throat
Of Brandywell, its floodlit dogtrack,
The throttle of the hare. In the first week
I was so homesick I couldn't even eat
The biscuits left to sweeten my exile.
I threw them over the fence one night
In September 1951
When the lights of houses in the Lecky Road
Were amber in the fog. It was an act
Of stealth.
        Then Belfast, and then Berkeley.
Here's two on's are sophisticated,
Dabbling in verses till they have become
A life; from bulky envelopes arriving
In vacation time to slim volumes
Despatched 'with the author's compliments'.
Your poems in longhand, ripped from the wire spine
Of an exercise book, bewildered me -
Vowels and ideas bandied free
As the wind's vowel in our sycamores.
I tried to write about the sycamores
And innovated a South Derry rhyme
With *hushed* and *lulled* full chimes for *pushed* and *pulled*.
Those hobnailed boots from beyond the mountain
Were walking, by God, all over the fine
Lawns of elocution.
        Have our accents
Changed? 'Catholics, in general, don't speak
As well as students from the protestant schools.'
Remember that stuff? Inferiority
Complexes, stuff that dreams were made on.
'What's your name, Heaney?'
                'Heaney, Father.'
                      'Fair

Enough.'
　　　　On my first day, the leather strap
Went epileptic in the Big Study,
Its echoes plashing over our bowed heads,
But I wrote home that a boarder's life
Was not so bad, shying as usual.

I came to life in troubled times (which ones?)
In the kissing seat of an Austin Sixteen
Parked at a gable, the engine running,
My fingers tight as ivy on her shoulders.
And heading back for home, the summer's
Freedom dwindling night by night, the air
All moonlight and a scent of hay, policemen
Swung their crimson flashlamps, crowding round
The car like black cattle, snuffing and pointing
The muzzle of a sten-gun in my eye:
'What's your name, driver?'
　　　　　　'Seamus ...'
　　　　　　　　　　Seamus?
They once read my letters at a roadblock
And shone their torches on your hieroglyphics,
'Svelte dictions' in a very florid hand.

Ulster was British, but with no rights on
The English lyric: all around us, though
We hadn't named it, the ministry of fear.

　　　　　　　　　　SEAMUS HEANEY

As a Child in Derry

As a child in Derry I heard the shots
And the crackle of burning timber
That signalled the ancient quarrel
Of Prod and Papist, that mindless feud
Lingering on in a lost province
Where memories of long-ago battles
Are as fresh as today's headlines.

Memories of siege and horror, of Lundy,
The Apprentice Boys and God-knows what
Fag-ends of ill-digested history
Make a stirring tale for children
But light the fuse in the bitter heart.

Tales of blood and sectarian thunder
Lead to a coarse and brutal logic
Where my side is whiter than white
And yours black as a raven's wing.

Once more the pogrom and police baton,
The mob's thick urgent cries,
The pool of blood in the doorway,
The incandescent blaze of hate.

Yet I who have gone away
To safe and easy exile
Cannot quite write them off
As simply ignorant thugs.

I too am involved in their crimes.

ROBERT GREACEN

Romanist

I was subjugated under arches, manumitted at a graduation ceremony, for years a humble client at the lattice of confessionals. My murex was the purple of lent on a calendar patterned with fish-days.
    I knelt to take the impress of the celebrant's ashy thumb, a silk friction, the spread palps of his fingers cold as mushrooms at my temples. An infinitesmal fall of dust itched down over my nose. Stipple of the first spadeful. *Momento homo quia pulvis es et in pulverem reverteris.*
    Caste-marked annually, I went among the freemen of the city for their inspection. In forum and theatre I felt their gaze bend to my mouldy brow and fasten like a lamprey on the mark. In vain I sought it myself on the groomed *optimi*, on the hammerheads of lictor and praetorian. I was estimated and enumerated with my own, indelibly one with the earth-starred denizens of catacomb and campagna.

SEAMUS HEANEY

Civil War
13 August 1970

The way I feel it coming
Is as a fire with one wing
That is already blackening
My heart;

Or as the blind hammering
Of the trapped crowd
On the closing walls
Of the street;

And the seams of the houses
Splitting in a swarm of cock-
Roaches that riot in an
Alarming silence;

And we are all running
Through a cloud, glimpsing icebergs,
Calling goodbye to disaster
And then hello;

The mirrors curl up like paper
In the rumpling fire;
Sightless we follow the blind
Whose hands

Drum fire from our brittle dread
Blow by saturating blow,
Until it hardens to a cold
Rallentando for the dead.

When it comes darkly over us
I will hold you and say
In disappointed love, 'Look
See my face in the wave?'

                SEAMUS DEANE

July

The drumming started in the cool of the evening
as if the dome of air were lightly hailed on.
But no. The drumming murmured from beneath that drum.
      The drumming didn't murmur, rather hammered.

Soundsmiths found a rhythm gradually. On the far
bench of the hills tuns and ingots were being
beaten thin.
The hills were a bellied sound-box resonating,
a low dyke against diurnal roar, a tidal wave
that stayed, that still might open.
Through red seas of July the Orange drummers
led a chosen people through their dream. Dilations
and engorgings, contrapuntal; slashers in shirt-
sleeves, collared in the sunset, policemen flanking
them like anthracite.
The air grew dark, cloud-barred, a butcher's
apron. The night hushed like a white-mothed reach
of water, miles downstream from the battle, skeins
of blood still lazing in the channel.

And so my ear was winnowed annually.

SEAMUS HEANEY

Reading Keats in Derry City

September deepens and the nights are long
And noisy; through this autumn damp with blood
There glows the other autumn of his song,
There falls the shadow of the old oak wood
Over the broken, dusty streets that lead
Us on to death's steep brink. And there is still
That spot where the sun slants across the hill
Burning the leaves as though the branches bleed.

My childhood's magic moments shone between
These ancient walls; I will return once more,
One evening late and weary I will lean
Against that gate or knock upon that door
To find again the dusky littered room
Where the oil lamp smokes and the curtains smell of home.

FRANCIS STUART

A Constable Calls

His bicycle stood at the windowsill, its fat black
handlegrips heating in sunlight, the 'spud' of
the dynamo gleaming and cocked back, the pedal

treads hanging relieved of the boot of the law.

His cap was upside down on the floor next his chair: the line of its pressure ran like bevel in his slightly sweating hair. He had unstrapped the heavy ledge and my father was making tillage returns in acres, roods and perches.

Arithmetic and fear. I sat staring at the polished holster with its buttoned flap, the braid cord lopped into the revolver butt.

'Any other root crops? Mangolds, marrowstems, anything like that?'

'No.'

But there was - that drill of turnips where the seed ran out in the potato field. I assumed small guilts and sat imagining the black hole in the barracks.

'Well, I'll have to be beating on.'

He stood up, shifted the baton case more accurately to his haunch, scabbarded and pocketed the fountain pen, fitted his cap back with two hands and looked at me for the first time when he'd said goodbye.

A shadow bobbed in the window as he clipped his trousers and snapped the carrier-spring over the leger. His boot pushed off and the bicycle ticked, ticked, ticked.

SEAMUS HEANEY

Thought on the Derry Riots

As I was walking round the streets of Derry
I saw old Hobbits
Looking very pleased.
He was wearing a policeman's hat
And about six watches
On his arm.
On his bicycle was
Half a landrover,
And in his hand
A bottle of wine.
I got to thinking there was a riot
And it looked as if old Hobbits had won.

ARTHUR McVEIGH

Hymn 1969
To the tune of 'Rise Up, O Men of God!'

Sit down, O men of God!
There is no need to stand;
Just take it easy, sit and wait,
Your placard in your hand.

Sit down and claim your rights,
Protest and demonstrate;
What you desire will in the end
Be handed on a plate.

Sit down, O men of God!
Your kingdom tarries long;
But sedentary brotherhood
Will pass the night with song.

So why then tire yourselves
By standing in the town?
Your strength proves equal to your task
And wins by sitting down.

Some strain you'll have to bear,
Tear-gas may make you weep;
But to reform the bad old world
The price you pay is cheap.

And if by sitting out
Climatic chills begin
To take their toll, you can achieve
As much by sitting in.

Authorities may then
Attempt to you dictate,
Cut light and heat, but sit you on,
Protest, participate.

Lift high your placard then.
Sit down where feet have trod.
A strummed guitar will overcome -
Sit down, O men of God!

                PATRIC STEVENSON

from No Truck

perhaps the first stone
was just a pebble
fallen off
a turning gravel truck
but it taunted
and so was thrown

the second
was an intent brick
apologist
of the first
once thrown
was soon returned
a pocked and bloody omen
more meaningful
than any word

then from alleyways forgotten
amid the derelict
          the old
abandoned antiques of broken
houses
          beams new piping
earmarked to carry discontent
away
          were ghosted rising
into barricades
at every minor exit's end

and so they came
long since prepared
wearing clothes for painting
or back yard chores
and broke new paving
for want of stone

spiriting petrol into glass
for example had taught them
that one man's temper
or the gout
of long dead kings
would call them to the barricades
again
while milk-men searched
the empty sills at dawn

knowing that their bottles
were becoming
           bombs

outside these barricades
            constabulary
donned the masks
of carrion ants
to clear their air
of life
like extinct creatures
whose cramping armoury
had long since caused
their inborn suicides
they hid their minds in steel
and charged
           hissing poison
into subtler faces
towards preconditioned eyes

the agony that was bottled up
for years
           burst flaming
on the ground
           and the weeping
that several decades had repressed
the gas induced
           with callous irony
top storeys which residents
had cursed
           with every stair
were now strong ramparts
           bastions
of high advantage

men used to throwing stones
at tins
           to pass the time
released a violence
           generations old
at fools
           who would repress them
yet again
           who didn't question
that the leaders
who now spurred them on
had sat unquestioning
much too long

50

you have baptised this vendetta
with water
you have anointed yourselves
with flame

    MICHAEL FRIEL

Bogside, Derry, 1971

Shielded, vague soldiers, visored, crouch alert:
between tall houses down the blackened street;
the hurled stones pour, hurt-instinct aims to hurt,
frustration spurts in flame about their feet.

Lads who at ease had tossed a laughing ball,
or, ganged in teams, pursued some shouting game,
beat angry fists against that stubborn wall
of faceless fears which now at last they name.

Night after night this city yields a stage
with peak of drama for the pointless day,
where shadows offer stature, roles to play,
urging the gestures which might purge in rage
the slights, the wrongs, the long indignities
the stubborn core within each heart defies.

    JOHN HEWITT

Trial Runs

WELCOME HOME YE LADS OF THE EIGHTH ARMY. There must be some defiance in it because it was painted along the demesne wall, a banner headline over the old news of *Remember 1690* and *No Surrender*, a great wingspan of lettering I hurried under with the messages.

  In a khaki shirt and brass-buckled belt, a demobbed neighbour leaned against our jamb. My father jingled silver deep in both pockets and laughed when the big clicking rosary beads were produced.

  'Did they make a papish of you over there?'

  'O damn the fear! I stole them for you, Paddy, off the pope's dresser when his back was turned.'

  'You could harness a donkey with them.'

Their laughter sailed above my head, a hoarse clamour, two big nervous birds dipping and lifting, making trial runs over a territory.

SEAMUS HEANEY

Another View of a Pig

A boar snouted
Beady eyed scavenger,
Slime green and stubby legged
With its cast iron skin;

Sightless at night
Prowling past
The shattered pod
Of a concrete tree
With a low deep throated
Growl,
As it smells
The fear and hatred
In its path.

MICHAEL BROPHY

Protest Poems

I   *Why the gun?*

Why must the gun be used?
Hatred, fear, reaction.
Why the gun?
From '98 to '74
The gun man standing by the door.

II   *Execution*

Our Trade Unionist friend
Strapped in a chair
Was carried out.
He is a soldier.
He stares ahead.
Pulls himself up:
'Aim! Fire!'

III *Remains*

Far removed the remains are from Murlough Bay.
    They lie in Glasnevin.
Hung for treason; picture his limp body,
       his twisted head.
          Returned to our shores in '65:
            'A mixture of Casement and Crippen'.

IV *Bernadette*

Irish passion unleashed.
The cry of an oppressed people.
The blood of Derry's 13 Dead.
The pulling of hair and battering by
The Cassandra of Cookstown.

V *Born into dying*

Despised, distrusted in our own land,
Denied freedom of procession
Under some one act or the other
We who put politicians into power
Born into pogroms
Not of our own making

And you ask us why
Violence rears its ugly head
Ask us who are
Born into dying

The dole-queue death.

                          GERRY LOCKE

Derry

I

The unemployment in our bones
Erupting on our hands in stones;

The thoughts of violence a relief,
The act of violence a grief;

Our bitterness and love
Hand in glove.

II

At the very most
The mind's eye
Perceives the ghost
Of the hands try
To timidly knock
On the walled rock
But nothing will come
And the hands become
As they must
Mailed fists.

III

The Scots and English
Settling for the best
The unfriendly natives
Ready for the worst.
It has been like this for years
Someone says,
It might be so forever, someone fears,
Or for days.

SEAMUS DEANE

Search

Soldiers in the hills now,
The jeep stops at the farm,
Beyond the fields, wind
Cuts its teeth on the rocks,
Light is acid, sun ashamed.
Over there in the pond
Newts pant, khakied, sullen,
Frogspawn sways, gangling -
Myriad eyes. Soldiers crawl
Down the hill, wind
Cuts its teeth on the rocks.

TERENCE BROWN

from Report of the Tribunal

This morning the buses were halted
on the road; a soldier came inside.
One joke, unanswered; read our faces
and left again.

And there we sat and smoked, told stories
of Glasgow, New York, the islands
off the Irish coast, about a pub
everyone knew.

Waited. The sound of our four tyres
in the rain, and the wind from the Lough
that came through the windows and froze us
into silence.

Nor did we move, when across the Foyle
Derry arose in the fog and fire's smoke;
Guildhall and Protestant Cathedral
guarding the wall.

Slowly the sun broke through as we crossed
the river, stopped at the checkpoint,
turned toward the derelict buildings and
burned out alleys ...

Hundreds of fathers out of work, stood
on a corner, Players Number 6
burning to the end of their fingers.
Stood and waited.

But not today. They were here. We jumped
out onto the road and saw thousands
ready to march, the blue Civil Rights flag
wet and wind-pulled ...

*   *   *   *

And fought each day, the boys leaving school,
'afternoon matinee,' stones and jeers,
hard joy, to meet bullet and the spray
of the battle.

Then, in the night, banging bin-lids and shouts
along William Street; crack of bullets
quick battles, and a friend rushed bleeding
into your room.

Tired now of that blood, neighbours met
in crowds and talked of sons in England,
married daughters and grandchildren
the cold afternoon.

Along the city walls, soldiers watched
like hunting birds, calling back and forth
along the air, smelt flesh and hair
and watched, waited

As we waited, bodies bundled tight,
the lines surging upon each other
like lovers, the fine sunshine and wind
upon our coats

So marched forward down William Street
to the Guildhall. We stopped, saw
barbed wire and rifles greeting us
as supplicants.

At the front, a steward raised his hands,
the crowd pressed forward, shouts; an old man
trying to move the wire stood laughing
at the blue steel ...

    * * * *

Then fired into the crowd, the rifles'
flash and their scarlet berets against
a sky turned grey once again. The crowd
turned, crouched, and ran;

moving blindly across the land torn up
for buildings, for planting grass when spring
or quiet gave us time; thought of faces
and dancing tunes.

And, out of breath, stopped and saw a woman
at her window, a child in brown shoes,
a girl with long hair tying a scarf
over her face.

A man, cigarette still caught between
his lips, shielded his mother and led
her away, she gripped a handkerchief
and prayed to God.

Down by Kells Walk, there was more shooting;
and west, at Glenfada, a long burst
and screaming. A boy fell
hard to the earth.

    * * * *

He lies still on the walk, one leg tucked
under the other, his tie still neat against
the white shirt. Some stones and rubble lie
not far away.

His mouth is open wide, as if to speak
once more. To say it never happened,
was a dream to keep for winter nights
before the fire.

Two men crouch to help a boy already
dead. His short jeans and jacket cover
his belly. The wound is too large,
crimson coloured.

The priests have anointed a dead man;
his blood spread out against the concrete
is covered over; the blue Civil Rights flag
red and wind torn.

And rain falls; you can see the swallows
in the fields, turning their bodies over
the world, to forget the earth and sun
to feel only wind.

TERENCE MAXWELL

After Derry 30 January 1972

Lightnings slaughtered
The distance. In the harmless houses
Faces narrowed. The membrane
Of power darkened
Above the valley,
And in a flood of khaki
Burst. Indigoed
As rain they came
As the thunder radioed
For a further
Haemorrhage of flame.

The roads died, the clocks
Went out. The peace
Had been a delicately flawed
Honeymoon signalling
The fearful marriage
To come. Death had been
A form of doubt.
Now it was moving
Like a missionary
Through the collapsed cities
Converting all it came among.

And when the storm passed
We came out of the back rooms
Wishing we could say
Ruin itself would last.
But the dead would not
Listen. Nor could we speak
Of love. Brothers had been
Pitiless. What could ignite
This sodden night?
Let us bury the corpses
Fast. Death is our future.

And now is our past.
There are new children
In the gaunt houses.
Your eyes are fused.
Youth has gone out
Like a light. Only the insects
Grovel for life, their strange heads
Twitching. No one kills them
Anymore. This is the honeymoon
Of the cockroach, the small
Spiderless eternity of the fly.

SEAMUS DEANE

Irish Dead

Under a lunar menses - kite and flame
Bleeding the old poisons like silver cess
Into the bright gutter of hell's new house -
The kern of my modern blood roots earth,
Kisses the lively dead, swoons to their slime,
And, mother-worm, murmurs name upon name.

We've picked the lock of time with an old bone,
Turned its tune and bowed the maggot's greed
Over each minted sun in a world's wood
Where the man-aping howler hugs his mate
And carrion young from the rite of spring;
But now we crouch in our kern's coffin's long

Shadow of red run live through every light:
Hell is now! The dead has burst its bag
Of tricks into today's full-throated blood.
Infected fire brands both the brothers killer.
Now the grim sardonic clowns unseat
Their audience and red mouths suck us white.

Our time is ever green. Here, through the eye
Of dust's hysteria, a green death climbs
Into our lap - its squint, its crooked limb,
Its wrinkled paw clawing out for the dug
Fellows to hoist their howl of mockery.
I'll write with a green stake. Our dead are spry.

PATRICK WILLIAMS

Apology

A town tolling bell, a fatal joke
that tells of
        maudlin pauses
in the heavy hours of rain, rings
every day.

Every day
        we spit on the diurnal slash
of the red morning wound
and in the day-long death throes
we fester

and I am ashamed to be human.

DENNIS KELLY

Two Psalms from Derry

Dante's city on a hill

In the wood of self-killers
trunks writhe: in particular
one with leaves blonde as tinder.
Slack skin crackles and her head
is lumped between her dry breasts.

Memory forces the chin up.
A pool of sky opens and
we see clouds but no matter.
Squad-cars police the nurseries;
the glass houses are barren.

A city set on a tomb,
though it hide, cannot be hid.
It has been dark these three days
after the last killings:
no stone rolled onto the void.

Under us, imagine fields
in the lower strata where
grain and bloom, root and climate
are all black soil, an empire
where the sun never rises.

A glass of winedreg remains;
two meat skewers from the last meal
lie across a plate. The drapes
are closed, velvet eyes under
a pelmet of gilded wood.

Already half William Street
must be imagined. Below
the bare clay with feet trampled
on it, a cold volcano
grows colder as it rises.

The seige

The emblem is made of jaws.
Closed it held a torch aloft
In a night of running skies
it snaps open with a sigh
like a pair of dividers.

Ironmongers mending the lamp
scarcely have time to notice
a girl's six-inch breasts, levelled
like pistols because of her
stomach which is full of blood.

As she imagines what soft
explosions they could have made
in her sweet, addled lake (oil
boiling in her clothes) the lamp
sunders with a squeal of flesh.

Food stores run out; a whole pig
floats away out of vision,
its throat cut like a red slice
of pineapple. The bridge brims
with water moving like skin.

     HUGH MAXTON

Derry Images, 1968-71

1

Derry, Londoned Derry, jerry-built
and gerrymandered - yet turning
to sky and mountain a profile spiritual
as one of its dark appealing ghetto-faces.

Close-up, eruptions of disease,
on dank walls, broken gable-ends:
'Up Paisley,' 'British Murderers,' 'Kick the Pope.'
What flowers among this detritus? -
slashing at nettles, a child runs barefoot begging.

2

A volley of bricks, stones, bottles -
loyal Fountain Street rips up a Civil Rights march.
From Ferryquay Gate, sealed three hundred years ago
by apprentices, their heirs the police
gaze over shields unstirred from duty:
keeping inviolate the Maiden City.

3

One comes back to the walls. A bastion overlooks
Nailors Row: rotten stumps like broken teeth
since they stoned the Catholics out of the street.

Roaring Meg still pokes a swart muzzle
at Creggan Heights where James's army stood.
Now houses mass up that slope.
'Those people all came from the mountains, with their priests.'

What walls out, binds in.
Even bible-drunk Walker, defender of the Siege,
is petrified turned inward: from his pillar
cannot see, on the road outside, his own slogan,
stolen to mock him: NO SURRENDER.

4

From the battlements by the Apprentice Boys' Hall girls flaunt
union jacks at the sullen Bogside below:
mean streets, men stood about on corners,
on the burroo, forced to cadge from their women who've jobs.
They stare back up the embankment, waiting
to come into their manhood, their split-level city.

7   (August 1969, the Battle of Bogside)

So I was there shooting,
with a camera. Images for cold storage. As:

armoured cars bludgeoning through a barricade
into a storm of petrol-bombs; veering deranged,
to limp back beaten like scorched insects;

scaffold-poles, concrete blocks, steel-reinforcing, built
into barricades - more urgent than houses;

teargas in the sun unrolling
like a voluptuous white carpet, beautiful -
at its touch men scattered like ashes;

night-skies aflame, like old film of the blitz in London;
and a hijacked Mr Softee ice-cream van
rolled blazing downhill at a mob,
chiming silvery as the moon - until the crash;

but especially a kind-faced man in a torn
sweater kissing his family goodbye after tea -
'No, you can't come with Daddy. Not till you're grown' -
as he set off, armed with dustbin-lid, stave.

Images: truths conserved; for sad ironic
collocation; from which to compose, elsewhere
at a desk, the lineaments of this time. But when,
I wondered on those frightened streets,

at what point of invasion reached, should I
have dropped my camera to throw stones, or run?
And which have done?

9   *(July 1971)*

Black flags, plaster saints, fresh flowers,
compose at the spot of death a noontide pause.
The shadow might be that pool of blood again.
It lengthens, steeping the violent evening.

These mourning-candles will light factories,
the tears wept fall as stones upon the soldiers.

10

A tensed land throbs to the Orange drums,
beaten till from burst veins blood runs,
till every ploughshare is a gun.

Romantic Ireland too lives on;
her crimsoned lips seduce; her tongue
knows no speech but bullet, bomb.

Hoarding a massive technology for killing,
troops tread the tripwired chequerboard; visored, wary,
aliens from a different planet.

ANDREW WATERMAN

I Used to Live

At Port-na-happle
where the happy people live
with their Atlantic view
and bone-handled knives
I dandered into wind
found sand dunes
cluttered with pagan trinkets
ancient gunballs warrior necklaces
and toward Foyle
heard someone rehearse
for real on a self-loading rifle
the day-doped dream
of getting shot-up

in this fear place
that looks out
on nothing
but
itself.

    GERALD DAWE

Fear

I used to smile
When people said
The heart stood still;
Until a midnight bell
Shrilled through the sleeping house
And unknown voices
Spoke beneath a window.
The very walls
Seemed to listen with me
Until a lock clicked;
And the strange car
Glided softly back
Into the darkness.

    ELEANOR MURRAY

Nothing but the Truth

Like the hero in an old-time novel
Who surrenders with his proud tortured smile,
Anxious to know the exact facts of betrayal,
I'll journey, tongue in cheek, joyously tossing
Perfect snowballs into time's furnace:

Youth's heroic vices and self inflicted legends,
All the Idea crushed to an embarrassing absurdity
By the mundane clash of knuckles on teeth:
A bloody-nosed snigger during the song of brotherhood!

    JAMES McFARLAND

The Other Side

I

Thigh-deep in sedge and marigolds
a neighbour laid his shadow
on the stream, vouching

'It's poor as Lazarus, that ground,'
and brushed away
among the shaken leafage:

I lay where his lea sloped
to meet our fallow,
nested on moss and rushes,

my ear swallowing
his fabulous, biblical dismissal,
that tongue of chosen people.

When he would stand like that
on the other side, white-haired,
swinging his blackthorn

at the march weeds,
he prophesied above our scraggy acres,
then turned away

towards his promised furrows
on the hill, a wake of pollen
drifting to our bank, next season's tares.

II

For days we would rehearse
each patriarchal dictum:
Lazarus, the Pharoah, Solomon

and David and Goliath rolled
magnificently, like loads of hay
too big for our small lanes,

or faltered on a rut -
'Your side of the house, I believe,
hardly rule by the book at all.'

His brain was a whitewashed kitchen
hung with texts, swept tidy
as the body o' the kirk.

III

Then sometimes when the rosary was dragging
mournfully on in the kitchen
We would hear his step round the gable

though not until after the litany
would the knock come to the door
and the casual whistle strike up

on the doorstep. 'A right-looking night,'
he might say, 'I was dandering by
and says I, I might as well call.'

But now I stand behind him
in the dark yard, in the moan of prayers.
He puts his hand in a pocket

or taps a little tune with a blackthorn
shyly, as if he were party to
lovemaking or a stranger's weeping.

Should I slip away, I wonder,
or go up and touch his shoulder
and talk about the weather

or the price of grass-seed?

SEAMUS HEANEY

Burnt Offerings

1

And now
that roar wells out
again,
filling the calescent stable;
as I lead him
tottering away
from the exquisite
neck and head,
turning to search me -
the eyes afterbirth pooling with loss,
the delicate supplication
of her folded hooves.

2

Finally unearthed,
　　　　one frantic hour later,
Enthroned between
　　　　coal-heap and bucket
Lost in the thrill
　　　　of the first kill -
A Daddy Long-leg's
　　　　deliberate dissection.
Each frail wing and leg
　　　　carefully plucked -
A wisping body
　　　　trapped in tiny finger-tips -
Until the final puzzlement
　　　　of nothing left.
Found - the head bowed uncertain.

3

When dawn eases
through the wire,
and pads along
the edge of your

inflicting snow:
I will come
with soup and bread
and valenkis dry;

to labour secretly
there by day -
to harvest the blossom
of your stubbly skull.

　　　　　　　　TOM McGURK

Docker

There, in the corner, staring at his drink,
The cap juts like a gantry's crossbeam,
Cowling plated forehead and sledgehead jaw.
Speech is clamped in the lips' vice.

That fist would drop a hammer on a Catholic -
Oh yes, that kind of thing could start again;
The only Roman collar he tolerates
Smiles all round his sleek pint of porter.

Mosaic imperatives bang home like rivets;
God is foreman with certain definite views
Who orders life in shifts of work and leisure.
A factory horn will blare the Resurrection.

He sits, strong and blunt as a Celtic cross,
Clearly used to silence and an armchair:
Tonight the wife and children will be quiet
At slammed door and smoker's cough in the hall.

SEAMUS HEANEY

Raid

The peacock stands above the farmyard muck,
Watching from the wall the leaf decked band

That waits in the lilac for the last attack,
Colder than the touch of rifles on bare hands,
Tired and sick - the air laden with lilac! -

Watching the peacock on the farmyard wall
Until he struts away, his tail grown dull.

CONLETH ELLIS

For Sean Cassidy, d. 24.2.1972

When you have everything,
When the high tense of your blood
Beats in your arms
And the steep migraine
Rises in salvoes
Of silence, when the unborn

Child stirs in the wet sling
Between the hunted bones,
Let there be murder in your eyes
For all betrayals,
Watch the stones

Become mossed in their treachery,
Keep the life up,
Startles the spies
Of conscience, catch the scouts
Of fear's army, be vigilant,

Watch the mysterious purity
Of love hinged on pain
Closing inward as gently
As the assassin's door
O Victim. Of all loneliness

There is no end. You must believe
To breed and kill more.
                    SEAMUS DEANE

The Hero
the phenomenon of the hero that like the salmon, he contributes to his own extinction

I   *the hero's salmon leap*

White with argument from the forenoon
Running from the courtroom grinning he

Is a living myth on acquittal from
'Smuggling arms' has had to live

Elsewhere if he wants to keep his bit
Of a family alive. There's his picture in the paper ...

What road is he taking in the long run
                but
Motors such high-jump leaps in the air
Skipping back down the law-court steps?

II   *the fiery salmon makes for himself a cold house*
                                             Ronan

His jaw is dark now and sets.

He's found a reason to kill, a 'cause'.

He's plotting murder, he forgets
Foot-free parish pantomime days

When he was the lad played Santa Claus.

                              PADRAIC FIACC

From Note on Passing

He is not purged
nor does he forgive himself
      or others
when the rifle goes off
or the milkchurn claymore
blasts a hole
in a border road.
      The white gelignite
does not, by its whiteness,
render him or others holy ...

    *   *   *

Those others
Those hundred human atoms
from Ballymurphy, Antrim,
Creggan, Cookstown,
the Falls; elsewhere.
      A friend,
a sister, the exploded skull
of a neighbour, strewn
in the roadway,
      led them here ...

    *   *   *

And if, in spring,
they pass on a street,
they must pass by.
No nod of head
      or wink of eye;
But a glance
      in a plate glass window
  or pool of water.
There is an RUC man
on the corner, hands
      in raincoat pockets,
a checkpoint down the street,
a patrol driving past,
      turret Browning
trained on his head ...

    *   *   *

He does what is needed to be done.
Keeping silent,

loitering around a corner,
covering a friend
             who ventures out
      to fire and run.
             He listens
for the signal
             of refuse bins
and whistles,
             retreats
to a doorway, knocks
and is let in.

There is no joy

only the sigh
of relief when the door closes
and he slumps into a chair.

He drinks tea
and listens for
             sounds in
the garden, the hallway, the street.

   * * *

He says, 'My nerves are shot.'
There is laughter for
- all their nerves - these bonded people
twist and are sharpened into a single blade;
and by that sharpness
             feel movements
in air, breathe, the eyes
             upon them.
(They are poised on their lives
and they must act.)

   * * *

When he is thrown
             against the wall
searched and questioned,
             he answers quickly;
feeling only the barrel
             like a hard punch
to the groin.
             He knows he will
get out. They will not find

the change,
        the hardness within him,
that reads the soldiers' eyes
        with a glance,
knows their thoughts
        and is safe.

        TERENCE MAXWELL

Guns for the Boys

The big man with the gun
Said
'I'm here to protect you.'
So he kicked me in the groin,
To show everyone his strength;

The small man with the gun
Said
'I'm here to protect you.'
So he burned the factory
Where I worked,
In case there was a sniper
On the roof;

The dark man with the gun
Said
'I'm here to protect you.'
So he knocked down my house
To get a clear field of fire;

Then the three men with their guns
Lined up
And shot me,
'You're easier to protect
When you're dead.'
They said.

        MICHAEL BROPHY

The Ballad of Ranger Best

You men of Ulster, can you spare the time
to think again about a last year's crime.
A boy killed on the 21st of May
by some Officials of the IRA.

I was in the Bogside where his corpse was found,
lying out on Sunday on some ruined ground.
We read the papers with strange dismay ...
a local fella from Rathkeele Way.

In '69 so his young friends said
he stood beside them at the barricade;
but he left his homeland for England's shore
as many an Irishman has done before.

He had no prospects that he could see,
but take the Queen's coin and go to Germany.
And then, his first stint of duty done,
come see his parents like a decent son.

Some British soldiers from the city wall
had shot a young boy out playing ball.
And so some armed Officials lay in wait;
by killing Best, they could retaliate.

He brought a friend home to the house for tea,
then said he had to call his fiancee.
And so a mother sees her youngster go.
Word of his death came on the radio.

It was on the twenty second of May
A statement issued by the IRA,
They had tried and sentenced young Ranger Best.
The Derry women then spoke out at last.

Two hundred women marched and came to stop
at Official headquarters in their little shop;
'We blamed the soldiers for what they do.
By that same token we are blaming you.'

'For Manus Deery we marched yesterday
down to the barracks of the soldiery.
We hardly care now who holds the guns,
we'll stand for nobody who kills our sons.'

Next day two thousand more began to shout,
'You can quit defending us from this day out.
We hate your coldness and hate your lies;
one death too many opened all our eyes.'

Oh Manus Deery and Ranger Best,
and Gerard Kelly and all the rest,

How many more will have died in vain
before our people live in peace again?

      JAMES SIMMONS

The Bomb Disposal

Is it just like picking a lock
with the slow deliberation of a funeral,
hesitating through a darkened nave
until you find the answer?

Listening to the malevolent tick
of its heart, can you read
the message of the threaded veins,
the chart of its body?

The city is a map of the city,
its forbidden areas changing daily.
I find myself in a crowded taxi
making deviations from the known route,

ending in a cul-de-sac
where everyone breaks out suddenly
in whispers, noting the boarded windows,
the drawn blinds.

      CIARAN CARSON

Claudy
A Ballad

The Sperrins surround it, the Faughan flows by,
at each end of Main Street, the hills' and sky,
the small town of Claudy at ease in the sun
last July in the morning, a new day begun.

How peaceful and pretty if the moment could stop.
McIlhenny is straightening things in his shop,
and his wife is outside serving petrol, and then,
a child takes a cloth to a big window-pane.

McCloskey is taking the weight off his feet,
and McClelland and Millar are sweeping the street,
and, delivering milk at the Beaufort Hotel,
young Temple's enjoying his first job quite well.

And Mrs McLaughlin is scrubbing her floor,
and Artie Hone's crossing the street to a door,
and Mrs Brown, looking around for her cat,
goes off up an entry - What's strange about that?

Not much - but before she comes back to the road
that strange car parked outside her door will explode,
and all of the people I've mentioned, outside,
will be waiting to die, or already have died.

An explosion too loud for your eardrums to bear,
and young children squealing like pigs in the square,
and all faces chalk white and streaked with bright red,
and the glass and the dust and the terrible dead ...

for an old lady's legs are ripped off, and the head
of a man's hanging open and still he's not dead.
He is screaming for mercy while his son stands and stares
and stares, and then, suddenly, quick, disappears.

And Christ! little Katharine Aikin is dead
and Mrs McCloskey is pierced through the head.
Meanwhile to Dungiven the killers have gone
and they're finding it hard to get through on the phone.

JAMES SIMMONS

Spotweld

Not a neighbourhood of fashion.
Curtains neat before the window, flowers
in flowerpots. The coal smoke falls
into the street and sits like a mist.
In the shop, a welder replaces sections
on farm machinery, calls to his helper,
who has gone to smoke in the doorway
and watch a girl pass on her way to school.
They say nothing. They smile.
He brings a cigarette to his mouth
and back down again. The smoke
comes out his nose.
A lorry passes between them.
By the time it moves on,
she has turned the corner.

He wants to go after her
but is held fast by his job
and the blast that hurls his ragged body
back into the shop.

    TERENCE MAXWELL

In this Year of Grace

The night-sky red, crackle and roar of flame,
the barricades across the ruined street,
the thump of stones, the shots, the thudding feet:
as mob greets mob with claim and counterclaim,
each blames the other, no one will accept the blame,
for fears entrenched will not permit retreat,
when creed and creed inhospitably meet,
and each child's fate's foreshadowed in its name.

So fare our cities in this year of grace,
sick with old poisons, seeped from history;
frustration on one side, the other fear
sodden with guilt. To their embattled place
the stubborn masters cling, while year by year
from this infection no man's blood runs free.

    JOHN HEWITT

Northern Ireland Late Night News

A rust red jelly
Darkening, thickening,
Congealing on the road;

The starhole in the windscreen
And a flourbag
Mark the spot;

And in an hour
When the clot

Has cracked and crumbled
The dried granules
Of a brain

Will be powder in the wind.

    MICHAEL BROPHY

A Slight 'Hitch'
March 1972

We wanted to think it was the quarry
but the pigeons roared with the white
smoke, black smoke, and the ghost

faced boy-broadcaster
fresh from the scene, broke down
into quivering lips and wild

tears. (can you imagine, and him
'live' on the TV screen!)

had to be quickly replaced
so that the News could be announced
in the usual cold, acid
and dignified way by the

Northern Ireland British
Broadcasting Corporation.

      PADRAIC FIACC

Derry Student Before and After

Before
in the derry night
I worried that I would be shot;
walking around with a guitar case
you might,
by either side;
(people have been killed
for less than this,
have they not?)

After,
in sunnyseethingfreezingcoldand damp portrush,
the world's troubles crackle from my radio
a one minute spot in the david hamilton show;
and ulster's latest bombing hardly rates
as much as fresh developments in the watergate;
a few seconds among top-twenty fun
that's the lot on radio one;
and in the 'sun'?
a paragraph,

'widowed mother's plea'
sandwiched tiny between
'party kiss that led to ducking'
and 'biggs goes free'.

sure, we have the concrete-filled
yellow and black drums here
in fact I've rather a large control zone sign
by my fire
but there's never any real sense of fear
you have to be fairly observant
to notice they're there;
and there's hardly any talk in pubs
of politics and bombs and such;

this bother's gone on too long, it's become a bore
though not to those involved, that's sure;
if it wasn't for the occasional
REALLY GORY MESS
we'd forget it, more or less -
what's a life and death matter in belfast
for us up here apart is a tea-time newscast,
like vietnam it at first appalled our senses
now we watch
and don't digest it.

          VICTOR THOMPSON

Third Movement: Belfast

Ballad to a Traditional Refrain

Red brick in the suburbs, white horse on the wall,
Eyetalian marbles in the City Hall:
O stranger from England, why stand so aghast?
May the Lord in His mercy be kind to Belfast.

This jewel that houses our hopes and our fears
Was knocked up from the swamp in the last hundred years;
But the last shall be first and the first shall be last;
May the Lord in His mercy be kind to Belfast.

We swore by King William there'd never be seen
An all-Irish Parliament at College Green,
So at Stormont we're nailing the flag to the mast:
May the Lord in His mercy be kind to Belfast.

O the bricks they will bleed and the rain it will weep,
And the damp Lagan fog lull the city to sleep;
It's to hell with the future and live in the past:
May the Lord in His mercy be kind to Belfast.

MAURICE JAMES CRAIG

Enemies

I

Belfast makes a tall boy
Bonfire for bonfirenight

To burn in effigy the guy
Calls himself a fellow Christ-
ian! The gall of this guy, we

Burn instead of crucify

Christ, the enemy ...

II

At the Gas and Electric Offices
Black boats with white sails

Float down the stairs
Frighten the five year old
Wee Protestant girls ...

'Nuns, nuns,' one of them yells
'When are yez gon' to git morried?'

      PADRAIC FIACC

Troubled City

In better days the road
Was lighted and night
Was as afternoon.
People shopped the road
And children counting
Cracks on paving stones
Skipped home from school.
And at night lamps
Gave like air to those
Travelling from dances
In the city centre
And the road never rested.

And then destruction came:
Slick-like, polluting
Her pavements, choking
All in its path
And even children, caught
In the darkness, died.
At night insecurity
Shuts out all light
And dawn is day
And troubled dusk.
Grief is counted on
Beads again and again.

      MICHAEL BOYLE

An Ulsterman (1969)

This is my country. If my people came
from England here four centuries ago,
the only trace that's left is in my name.
Kilmore, Armagh, no other sod can show
the weathered stone of our first burying.
Born in Belfast which drew the landless in,
that river-straddling, hill-rimmed town, I cling
to the inflexions of my origin.

Though creed-crazed zealots and the ignorant crowd,
long nurtured, never checked, in ways of hate,
have made our streets a by-word of offence,
this is my country, never disavowed.
When it is fouled, shall I not remonstrate?
My heritage is not their violence.

                                            JOHN HEWITT

From Belfast 1964

Coffin lids of unconcern, screwed down, when
Pigeons clatter from the charred lopped trees
Where children chatter along terraced streets -
Their heritage grime-stuccoed slate and brick.

Skeleton woman, we will sleep while you bear
Your child starved dead in a rag in your arms,
Your frozen breath masking your face ... No hope!

Bus burns and Belfast burns; shop windows crash,
And hope of closing wounds and oneness - despair!

Autumn comes to Divis Street in splintered glass,
Twisted gratings, stones and hurleys; grass
Behind the railings of Saint Comgall's strewn
With shrivelled leaves; outside - because a tune,
A phrase, a flag can strangle rote-learnt grace

Find splintered, shrivelled heart and twisted face!

Is it in me, this pain, or in this place (or) both?

                                    CONLETH ELLIS

Son of a Gun

> *'Woe to the boy*
> *for whom the nails,*
> *the crown of thorns,*
> *the sponge of gall*
> *were the first toy.'*   *François Mauriac*

Between the year of the slump and the sell-out, I
The third child, am the first born alive ...

My father is a Free Stater 'Cavan Buck'.
My mother is a Belfast factory worker. Both

Carry guns, and the grandmother with a gun
In her apron, making the military wipe

Their boots before they rape the house. (These
Civil wars are only ever over on paper.)

Armed police are still raping my dreams
Thump-thud. Thump-thud. I go on nightmaring

Dead father running. There is a bull
In the field. Is father, am I, running away

From the bull to it? Is this the reason why
I steal time, things, places, people?

Bar-man father, sleeping with a gun under
Your pillow, does the gun help you that much I wonder

For the gun has made you all only the one
In of sex with me the two sexed son (or three

Or none) you bequeathed the gun to
Still cannot make it so. I can

Never become your he-man: shot
Down born as I was, sure, I thought

And thought and thought but blood ran ...

PADRAIC FIACC

English Class

Weep far away, quietly,
Slum child; beauty
From a distance I read
At you - Reeves and
Farjeon: do not involve
Me.
   Fifteen is coming -
Mill then and courting,
Terrace home, ugliness,
Red grave and a white
Cross facing the motorway -
Do not involve me,

Slum child. Why must you
Bring me your poems scrawled
On the back of your mind?

                    CONLETH ELLIS

Dance Little Man

They said 'Dance little man,'
So I danced,
And I smiled as they smiled
And enjoyed the ordeal.

Then they said, 'Cry little man,'
So I cried,
And the tears they were real,
Because it was love I had lost;

And the more that I cried
The more they would laugh,
Then they said, 'Sing little man,'
So I sang tham a sad song;

But they said, 'No! no! little man,
A gay song, a happy song';
So I sang them their song,
And enjoyed the ordeal.

                    MICHAEL BROPHY

I Won't Dance

I am of Northern Ireland: born
Behind a barricade where trenched
Soldiers shot from our front garden
Eavesdropping snipers without grief or pardon.

In 1905 a geordie girl
Came pinafored to Belfast school;
Grew up with Belfast prod and mick;
Renounced the Second English war, then, sick,

Died in the rubble of her world.
The chip I shoulder is one half
Belfast-Irish, English part
My mother's broken nonconforming heart.

If I bequeath to girl and son
An old song rubbed by fiddler's thumb,
A greying protest, I mind green
Famine mouths that hawked alone
Over shrivelled roots and snarls,
Cracked dung, ancestral crawling things -
And dead men crouched on calloused hands
That wrought an absent God's rent, racked townlands.

I am of Northern Ireland: born
Behind a mattressed window when
The crossfire between love and hate
Jerked a corpse across our garden gate:

Where introverted streets divert
Highways to culdesacs and all
My constitutionals end with
The dead man on the gate and in the myth.

I am of Northern Ireland: born
To exile in a local street
When only bullets danced at night
And death scared skipping children from the gate.

                              ROY McFADDEN

The British Connection

In Belfast, Europe, your man
Met the Military come to raid
The house:

'Over my dead body
Sir,' he said, brandishing
A real-life sword from some
Old half forgotten war ...

And youths with real bows and arrows
And coppers and marbles good as bullets
And old time thrupenny bits and stones
Screws, bolts, nuts, (Belfast confetti)

And kitchen knives, pokers, Guinness tins
And nail-bombs down by the Shore Road

And guns under the harbour wharf
And bullets in the docker's tea tin
And gelignite in the tool shed
And grenades in the scullery larder
And weed killer and sugar
And acid in the french letter

And sodium chlorate and nitrates
In the suburban garage
In the boot of the car

And guns in the oven grill
And guns in the spinster's shift

And ammunition and more more
Guns in the broken down rusted
Merry-Go-Round in the Scrap Yard

Almost as many hard-on
Guns as there are union jacks.

     PADRAIC FIACC

Cave

The rifled honeycomb
of the high-rise hotel
where a wind tunnel moans.
While camouflaged troops
ransack the Falls, race
through huddled streets,
we lie awake, the wide
window washed with rain,

your oval face, and tide
of yellow hair luminous
as you turn to me again
seeking refuge as the
cave of night blooms
with fresh explosions.

    JOHN MONTAGUE

The Kickers

I

Glowing with the school-empty screech
Of a flock of heady girls - men

With penny coloured brief eyes
Like pearls on the skin of the new-born

Climb the heavy with childhood hull
Hang on to the anchor-chained walls

Wave flags over Belfast on fire
Afraid of the gale-torn posters on

The empty lot hoardings would whip
The feet from under them,
    'Kick King Billy
On the bum' and or 'Kick
The Pope' (thon whore of Babylon!)'

Kick the kick of the hanging man
From pawn to pub from pub to pawn.

II

Tell thin layer of earth-capped skull
Red with the fire of clay in slime

Befriending the other in a ditch
Which the stranger which the brother

Hundreds of years later when
Office girls giggle with nerves at the look

Of the labouring man, himself took sick
By 'queer fumes', throws up on

All the land the king owns and kicks
The bones
        out of the way of mounting bricks.

III

'It was our icons not
our guns you spat on'

Far away in the night
Though never all that far

The Military and/or Police
Are kicking down the door

Of a small kitchen house
Holding young babies up
        by the feet

Shaking them for guns
Turning the dead over
        in their coffins

To search under the bones
Find nothing but their own

Shit from the night before
When they dossed down in some

Old creature's parlour
And used it like the poor

Brutes we all still are
Kicking in the womb.

                PADRAIC FIACC

Dark Night of the Mill Hag

She shrieks like a bird hiccuping

'I was the Chief Bombadier ...
We fought the Battle of Seaforde Street.
In my day I did my stint.
I organised the Turning Over of the Tram
Full of them Shipyard monkies
Coming home from holding

The heads of Catholic workers
Down in the water till their lungs burst ...

A party of a hundred women or so
Led on by myself!

Nor did we ask them to get out first!'

(On the landing, an oil lamp in her fist,
Ready to plunge the house on fire!)

'In my day there was nothing but the cream
Of Ireland's men in the IRA!
Nothing now but empty
Skites, knaves, "craters"
Leading double lives, more faces
On them than the Town Clock!'

She said she saw a man's head pass by
The second storey window.

'Och not a 'tall gran'-ma
Or else he'd be an awful long
John Silver!'
        Then the lamp was hurled
And geranium pot after geranium pot
Before, whoever it was, could
Find her a bed in the Asylum from
Childhood to childhood
        in a world-

Womb to womb: to womb-removed.

                PADRAIC FIACC

Old Men's Letters

Now that two storey Tiger's Bay
(bog in the back)
hovels are gone,
the bricks made ballast
for some push into the harbour;
the markets dead,
the noisy dealers of
fruit, fish, and old clothes
buried or pensioned off

to prowl the streets,
bothering children's play
with their slow precarious way of walking,
We say, 'Turn back.'
Strange, like Cu Chulainn's
bloody sword that would not
come clean in drowning.
His son's body a strainer,
holes full of congealed bitterness.

And though we mutter
Our protests like prayers,
leaning down by an old bridge
or a hedge full of yellow gorse,
intoning in hoarse pentameters
the canticles of nature;
tall buildings, wide streets,
the moan of a thousand machines
clattering over stones
cross us.

A worker, his pint before the box,
stripping the day
to sleep full-bellied at night,
(when his grandfather
- tenant farmer -
turned the earth
with fuck all in sight but question marks)
waves our intellectual regrets away
and grabs his wife,
who drops Cu Chulainn's knife.

TERENCE MAXWELL

Linen

From the photographs of bleach-greens
Mill-hands stare across the snowy acres.
In a frieze white as marble
Their lives are ravelled and unravelled -
Golden straw, bright thread, the iron looms
Are cast in tangled cordage.

The shapes of wheels and spindless shine
In darkness. When the weave is finished,
Light will fall on linen simply, as it would

On glass, or silverware, or water,
Things needed for a wedding or a funeral;
We will be reconciled to those cold sheets.

     CIARAN CARSON

Christ Goodbye
Or how we turn Christ into an 'inhuman martyr' in Belfast

I

Dandering home from work at mid
-night, they tripped Him up on a ramp
asked Him if He were a 'Catholic' ...

A wee bit soft in the head He was,
the last person in the world you'd want
to hurt:
   His arms and legs, broken,
His genitals roasted with a ship
-yard worker's blow lamp.

II

In all the stories that the Christian Brothers
tell you of Christ He never screamed
like this. Surely this is not the way
to show a 'manly bearing'
screaming for them to PLEASE STOP!
and then, later, like screaming for death!

When they made Him wash the stab
wounds at the sink, they kept on
hammering Him with the pick
-axe handle; then they pulled
Christ's trousers down, threatening to
'cut off His balls'!
   Poor boy Christ, for when
they finally got round to finishing Him off
by shooting Him in the back of the head

'The poor Fenian fucker was already dead!'

     PADRAIC FIACC

Ulster Ritual

Alone now
As Christ if twelve
Loves were untrue,
Dark we walk
In the dead weight
Of congealed light.
I know we know
TV and chair,
A good fire,
Smiles out of doors
In a smooth street,
No immaculate
With tea at six -
No pill like that.
But a dream of nails
And vinegar
Waters the mass
Grave we farm;
Streets buckle and
We scream in the night;
A black root
Stirs in the earth -
A cross sprouts.
And we are the nails
And the Victim. We
Call to the Father
Who must not answer,
And circle ourselves -
Jeering.

      PATRICK WILLIAMS

Peter

As I denied his name
Like a coxcomb of embroidery
Unpicked from a silken vestment,
My judges would deny me

Such common dialects of death
As pitch-cap; rack; the wooden coffin
With its wedges hammered in
To crush the bone like so much chalk;

The stump of a tongue
Wagging - the agony of those
Who hold his syllables in parenthesis.
Or, lashed to the cannon's mouth,

What I had been would unclench into absence
Before the sound had pierced my ear-drums:
In flecks, in cords and twists
My being scattered,

Sifted through the universe
Like cotton waste. If his grace should be a mill
In which the damned are charred,
Shaped, and woven into something new,

Let me be strapped to the wheel,
Roped over the cross-beam of forged iron
Like the tongue slats
Held beneath the sliver leash.

Let my wounds cloud their red milk
Through the water - the instant blossom
On a linen bandage, falling
And ascending, dissolving with my name.

CIARAN CARSON

The Ballad of Gerry Kelly, Newsagent

Here's a song for Gerry Kelly,
listen carefully and see
what's the moral of the story.
It makes no sense to me.

Worked ten hours six days a week,
Sundays closed at three.
They say he made a decent living.
Rather him than me.

Social centre for the neighbours -
not much cash in that -
buying fags or blades or tissues,
waiting on to chat.

Sixty nine the nightmare started,
Loyalist anger rose;

sweet shops, butcher shops and pubs
were burned down, forced to close.

Who'd believe who never saw it ...
the broken glass, the noise,
voices shouting, 'Fenian bastard.'
- little Ulster boys?

Down the hill of lies and horror
Belfast city slipped.
Twice the Tartan thugs came for him,
robbed and pistol-whipped.

Standing in his shattered shop
and taking inventory
of loss and damage, Gerry Kelly
longed to get away.

Who would buy the ruined business
that he'd worked to build?
No one, so he waited, hoping
until he was killed.

One dark evening last November -
turn the lights on till we see -
Gerry Kelly still in business,
wife gone back to make the tea.

Sorting out the evening papers
while his son is selling sweets,
in our time, our town, two gunmen
walk in off the streets.

JAMES SIMMONS

As It Should Be

We hunted the mad bastard
Through bog, moorland, rock, to the starlit west
And gunned him down in a blind yard
Between ten sleeping lorries
And an electricity generator.

Let us hear no idle talk
Of the moon in the Yellow River;
The air blows softer since his departure.

Since his tide-burial during school-hours
Our kiddies have known no bad dreams.
Their cries echo lightly along the coast.

This is as it should be.
They will thank us for it when they grow up
To a world with method in it.

DEREK MAHON

Black Hole
A mental illness gives 'X' a youthful appearance; he's mistaken by the Military for a youth and dragged to the Barracks.

Eyes running together
want to, screaming, meet
each other, forge and fuse
into one
head-splitting frown
cannot shut:
         I am
this wild wide open
hysterical as a woman
man.

Some one kicks me in
'The Temple of
The Holy Ghost' and when
I fall
         pees
across my eyes
(shut hard tight as
a dead bird's.)

The RUC man says
'For Christ's sake
He's over forty!'
would guard
me against a colour
of black I never
believed existed.

Sometimes when I waken
from a nightmare of being
dead now
there is no God

at this end of that
black. No God, no man
just my two eyes
wanting to fuse into one
and cannot
         shut
even when
I shut them.

        PADRAIC FIACC

Ghosts

I am haunted by ghosts:
not headless phantoms,
nor knights hollow within their iron,
but ghosts of children.

Their eyes glitter from the splintered glass,
their bones rattle in shuttered windows,
their flesh cries from the pulp
of the bookstall bombed last week.

Worst are the living children
who advance, stones at the ready,
uttering this week's obscenities
from lips still wet with mothers' milk.

I mourn - as yet - no private ghost.
I am the 'moderate' whose voice
is drowned out by bomb-blast.
I am haunted by lost children.

        META MAYNE REID

Kids at War

I

Irish kids sneer and jeer
At, salute with cat
calls the dead body
Of the young British soldier

Gave up his life to save
The Irish women and kids

Caught in the Spring-
field Road Barracks
About to explode ...

II

The half-kid British soldier
On Lolly Pop Duty day
Strolls
Into the sweet shop to buy
The Irish kids ice-lollies
Is shot dead
By an Irish kid
Waiting outside
(The one whose head
He rolled his cap on.)

   PADRAIC FIACC

Wounds

Here are two pictures from my father's head -
I have kept them like secrets until now:
First, the Ulster Division at the Somme
Going over the top with 'Fuck the Pope!'
'No Surrender!': a boy about to die,
Screaming 'Give 'em one for the Shankill!'
'Wilder than Gurkhas' were my father's words
Of admiration and bewilderment.
Next comes the London-Scottish padre
Resettling kilts with his swagger-stick,
With a stylish backhand and a prayer.
Over a landscape of dead buttocks
My father followed him for fifty years.
At last, a belated casualty,
He said - lead traces flaring till they hurt -
'I am dying for King and Country, slowly.'
I touched his hand, his thin head I touched.

Now, with military honours of a kind,
With his badges, his medals like rainbows,
His spinning compass, I bury beside him
Three teenage soldiers, bellies full of
Bullets and Irish beer, their flies undone.
A packet of Woodbines I throw in,
A lucifer, the Sacred Heart of Jesus

Paralysed as heavy guns put out
The night-light in a nursery for ever;
Also a bus-conductor's uniform -
He collapsed beside his carpet-slippers
Without a murmur, shot through the head
By a shivering boy who wandered in
Before they could turn the television down
Or tidy away the supper dishes.
To the children, to a bewildered wife,
I think 'Sorry Missus' was what he said.

      MICHAEL LONGLEY

Live Games
for Brian

Kids down on hunkers
crawling through
the brickworks with
woodguns the big
brother done on
the backhut lathe
spring up and shout:
'Da da you're dead!'
and by
the stinking river
they jamjar spricks
a wee lad's body
has been dumped
shot through the head.

   GERALD DAWE

Childrens' Games

Looking out across the playground,
tarmac black with railings sharp
as soldiers' spikes,

I see the children caught like leaves
amongst the stirring winter here,
falling, tumbling, shrieking, frightened
clinging, to each other as they fall -

At times like these in Yorkshire,
I would count the children dead from war:
when the earth moved and they fell,
their broken bits of body tumbling, floating

in a soldier's deepening eye.

SHAUN TRAYNOR

A Soldier's Son
for Andrew

A young man's war it is, a young man's war
Or so they say and so they go to wage
This struggle where, armoured only in nightmare,
Every warrior is under age,
A son seeing each night leave as father
A man who may become the ancestor

In a backstreet, stabbing, at a ghetto corner,
Of future wars and further fratricide.
Son of a soldier who saw war on the ground
Now cross the peace lines I have made for you
To find on this side if not peace then honour,
Your heritage, knowing as I do

That in the cross hairs of his gun he found
You his only son and when he aimed
And when the bullet cracked the only sound
Was of his son rifling his heart. You twist
That heart today; you are his killed, his maimed.
He is your war; you are his pacifist.

EAVAN BOLAND

Enemy Encounter
for Lilac

Dumping (left over from the autumn)
Dead leaves, near a culvert
I come on
        a British Army Soldier
With a rifle and a radio
Perched, hiding. He has red hair.

He is young enough to be my weenie
-bopper daughter's boy-friend.
He is like a lonely little winter
        robin.

We are that close to each other, I
Can nearly hear his heart beating.

I say something bland to make him grin
But his glass eyes look past my side
-whiskers down
        to the Shore Road street:
I am an Irish man
        and he is afraid
That I have come to kill him.

                PADRAIC FIACC

Ulster 71
'Ulster is the safest place in the world to have a heart attack.'
                Information Recording: 'Ulster 71'

To this land of postponed death
A played out blown back citizen
Accumulates, obelisk, on the quay
Because the tv smiling adverts
Stilled his early coronary fear:

'Come home to have your heart-attack here!'

Behind the new-enshrined living
They proclaim a limbo of wonder
To god and resurrected magnates
Yet the holy war struggles on; many
Faced with fatality and incubus,
Race round the streets in which
No-one may depart life
        naturally!

                DENNIS KELLY

From The Women's Tale
(Impressions on a BBC programme, 20 March 1974)

I ranged Donegall Street, she said
Till a bin-mate sided his head
To say: Hospital. I knew he meant: Dead.

The house became empty first,
Then a day was hollow
Like each day that would follow.
Now nights are worse.
Sometimes in the morning
I startle to hear him returning.

My hardest task
Is when the children ask.

For one: The twins haven't even an ember
Of him to remember.
For another: It's gall
To hear them tell things he said, did, I can't recall.

Yes, he has senses, he hears,
She speaks against tears,
He seems to know what I say,
He blinks and peers.
If the people who murder and maul
Could see what they did to our Paul

So butchered so small.

As he grows need increases:
I mustn't go to pieces.
Until eight or nine
A mother does fine
But a father is needed then
To shape boys into men.
I can't give the discipline.
At Christmas for a toy
I know what a girl will enjoy
But what's right for a boy?

One, in the last take,
Bitterness still at bay,
Saying, I must make
A show for the children's sake,
And smile whatever comes up, sounded brave, almost gay,
But, passing along with her pram, she was facing away.

WILLIAM J PHILBIN

Tears
for Joseph Parker

I   *Unisex*

After the bombing the British soldier
Looks up into the barbwired Irish
Twilight. His unflinching open eyes
Deaden, yet involuntarily flood
With the colour of tea
Drenches his combat jacket sleeve.

Now he is hugging,
Now he is giving
           his male love
To a screaming fellow being, he does
Not know if it is a man or a woman.

II   *What price peace?*

Nine years of age, on the bus:
         like a baby
Inside of her, crying

The length of a life time's journey ...

Not that she 'lost' her penny
But that it was 'stolen' ...

The Conductor said 'Quit blurtin' love!
I let you on without the penny, didn't I?
A penny isn't worth blurtin' for.'

But nobody can stop the long thin crying

For nobody saw her the day the men
Were that busy holding back the women
They forgot about the kids

The day she ran up the street alone
To the still smouldering (like peat) pub:
Somebody younger than nine years of age

Watching them dig from the wreckage.

III   *Lullaby*

When the ricocheting bullet bites into

The young child who wanted to walk
In her mother's high heels to push
The doll's pram, she gives out

A funny little 'oooh!'
And lets the blood spill
All over her bright new bib ...

No pallbearers are needed.

The young father is able himself to carry
The immaculate white coffin but
Stains it with a dirtyfaced boy's
Fist-smudged tears
        then suddenly cries
Out like a man being tortured by water.

                PADRAIC FIACC

Falls Funeral

Unmarked faces
fierce with grief

a procession of children
led by a small coffin

the young
mourning the young

a sight beyond tears
beyond pious belief

David's brethren
in the Land of Goliath.

           JOHN MONTAGUE

Child of our Time
for Aengus 17. 5.74

Yesterday I knew no lullaby
But you have taught me overnight to order
This song which takes from your final cry
Its tune, from your unreasoned end its reason,

Its rhythms from the discord of your murder,
Its motive from the fact you cannot listen.

We who should have known how to instruct
With rhymes for your waking, rhythms for your sleep,
Names for the animals you took to bed,
Tales to distract, legends to protect,
Later an idiom for you to keep
And living, learn must learn from you, dead,

To make our broken images rebuild
Themselves around your limbs, your broken
Image, find for your sake whose life our idle
Talk has cost, a new language. Child
Of our time our times have robbed your cradle,
Sleep in a world your final sleep has woken.

EAVAN BOLAND

Three Year Old: Belfast 1972

She scarcely speaks,
wakes in the night screaming.

Yet she was fortunate
when the street exploded into flame.
She only took one bruise
though Mother was thrown to the wall,
the basket whirled into nothingness,
and the pram was crushed.

Now she expects
the whole world to explode again:

She hides her eyes and stares
into her bomb
-blasted imagination.

META MAYNE REID

The Snatch

It seemed such a cheap
Stage effect of reality that Death
Hiding in the wings

On a foundry roof
Sniping at soldiers, should
Like a childless woman,
Snatch away
A wee chalk-faced boy
Playing marbles in the mud.

    PADRAIC FIACC

For Giles Gordon

The sun may shine even on a child's coffin.
  The south wind will caress
the man who has forgotten joy
gently as it kisses the love-linked
love-lost couple in the wood.
On prison camp, or on the ruined walls
the fireweed flares in conflagration
of sharp fire.

Only our eyes change, our ears grow deaf,
our hearts break, or dance, or die.
But the sea flows, and the indifferent wave
passes and pauses, coiling and recoiling
constant in its own change,
free of the fickle weather of the heart
which clouds or gloriously creates our day.

    META MAYNE REID

Kindertotenlieder

There can be no songs for dead children
Near the crazy circle of explosions,
The splintering tangent of the ricochet,

No songs for the children who have become
My unrestricted tenants, fingerprints
Everywhere, teethmarks on this and that.

    MICHAEL LONGLEY

Riot

Pink of a broken cherry-spray
dropped by the hospital drive
: pink and white

                the mercurochrome
smeared still, dripped
about the bandages   shoulder's paleness

those blossoms
lying in strange stillness   the branch-sliver

his eyes screaming

          *   *   *

Two small girls
were playing tig near a car ...

How many counties, would you say,
are worth their scattered fingers?

                    DESMOND EGAN

Rites

I   *This is my fear*

this is my fear
that I who have observed
the beauty of an insane woman
time after time, appear
to imitate her ritual; the water
she has carried within
cupped hands,
I cannot hold. Into the thin
and delicate vessel of poetry,
live water spills.

II   *None*

What requiem shall the Choir sing?
Other than the need to overcome despair,
Somehow to give order to this thing,
What use our ritual? What prayer

Could exorcize ghosts buried in
The conscience of this city? At night gunpowder
Flames above the asphalt. Only the sirens sing.

PAUL MURRAY

Dying Truth

There she stood,
Stark against the dark velvet sky,
Etched in red, by the glowing fires
That were burning in the bowels
Of this stricken edifice,
Whose staring empty sightless windows
On being drained of their strength,
Cracked, and crashed into the street below
Sending men scurrying for safety.
This was the day long pattern
To the wet, weary beleaguered firemen,
Who, unaware that above,
Hidden in the crimson sky,
The Angel of Death was spreading her wings
Over the Holocaust below.
A rumbling crash heralds the sound of tragedy.
Cold sickening fear grips the heart
As the injured are removed.
A sigh of relief:
(Although hurt, and bloodied, they are alive!)
The building, rent and torn
Open to the night sky
With laths and beams
Is standing in all manner of grotesque poses.
It's here amid the rubble
One had the feeling of an interloper
Who had breached a sacred moment in life:
Inside the remains of the citadel
This bastion of the Salvation Army,
Here by the pale light of lamps,
A group of sweating, panting men worked
To free a suffering fellow human being.
How long they worked, no one knows
For time has no meaning in moments like these
And as one's gaze wanders around
The remains of this holy place.
A whisper like the sighing of a gentle breeze was heard:
'She's dead!'

God was now in the presence of this assembly
Who silently mourned the passing
Of a loved Salvationist
And many eyes looked at the remaining wall
With its painted emblem
And the words 'Blood and Fire'.

W T STEVENSON

A Lack of Beauty in our Lives
song from the play 'Ulster Lies Bleeding'

a lack of beauty in our lives
the spark that drives
through dark of day
to make it glow
a rusty mind
no sweetness find
to make it flow
a rising ground
where freedom's found
and love unbound
        now mixed with science
our tree might grow.

young couple murdered in a cab
they did not know
their tender night would end in blood
the taximan conceals a gun -
        a racist hood
in the backseat there
he shoots his fare
        then leaves his taxi-rank of hate
and hastens home.

JAMES McKENNA

Summer 1970

It is the season of death,
furred, feathered things crushed to the roads,
insects smacking themselves
to pulp on the windscreen, and
the bulldozer gouging back
ditch, hedgerow, root and branch:

gashed green bleeds red soil.
'Community Relations Committee
campaigns to keep temperature down';
but in town after little town
strident with union jacks
riding its fields afloat
on tidal flute and drum
the heat beats up. The road
dips from the hills into
the hazed pit of Belfast,
an army-truck gouts black smoke
over late-flowering thorn;
the sniper climbs to his roof,
wall blazoned 'One man one gun'.

     ANDREW WATERMAN

Rat's Lot

Once, under a haystack, young rats,
Fat and pink like uncooked cocktail sausages
The farmer skewered them, warm and breathing, on a pitchfork.

And there was an old griddle by the water-barrel,
Spread thick and slimy with bird-lime.
I, a child, watched from a distance the stuck rat struggling.
On the second day hunger-fury burned in its eyes.
The child threw cheese secretly, and slept that night.
In the morning, rat was glued, mouth-down.

They kept it in a cage for maybe three days.
It had learned to stop lurching against the wire -
To stop gnawing - and wait.
When the cage opened it was too wise or too weak to move.
They prodded its convex back and it flew in fear.
Poor rat hadn't a chance - the terrier's jaws were waiting.

Rats come starving up from the river in winter -
Fill their bellies with oatmealish poisoning.
Back to the water, the first sip explodes them.

Rat-guts, flesh-pink and bloodless, skidded over a wet road.
Skin, like a child's sogged fur mitt; tail,
Bony, whippity and dead.

     JOAN NEWMANN

The Wrong Ones
for Desmond

The howl of the rain beating on the military tin
Roof is like the tolling of a bell
Tolling for a childhood more
Murdering than murdered.

I rise and stalk across the scarred with storm-
erected daisies, night in the north, grass.

My water-coloured twilit-childhood island-
scape is barricaded with circles of rain-rusted
Orange, coiled to kill, barbed wire.

Behind the corrugated iron walls of the Barracks
Dead mother rises again to bang bin lids
On dark mornings to warn husband and sons:
'The Pigs, the Pigs are coming!'

The air is filled with shooting, the sky
The colour of smoke, wends across the soot
-stained grass, the grey Belfast wind
Is blowing against the unblooming-as-yet wall
-flower mind. I reach my hand out and touch
Two hundred years old iron and chipped brick.

I'll be a 'son of a gun' forever now.
Forever now I'll never be right, I'm one
Of the Wrong Ones: No one will help
The grim faced teenaged British soldiers or young
Cops, hating the being hated; we all
Go down the road now as sharp and small
As razor blades:
        I pick my steps across
My backstreet childhood as a soldier would pick
His steps across a little mine-filled field.

                      PADRAIC FIACC

Heil Hitler

The path of reason's very safe
As I was taught. But I remember best
When Hitler Coyle broke into school
And shit upon the teacher's desk.

They labelled him a filthy coward,
His low action worse than stealing.
Punishment was suitably severe
From fear of such contempt, such feeling.

I though it funny, even brave,
But didn't say. I lack conviction,
Taught this timid reasonable touch,
Castrated early on by education.

So help me, hooligans and blackguards all,
Your huge hands itching for the kill.
I'll indicate what ballsed us up
And you can settle it, as you will.

                    MICHAEL FOLEY

Experience

'I want to fight you,' he said in a Belfast accent.
Amazed and scared, with hurried words I resisted.
'Fighting solves nothing. Tell me how I've annoyed you,'
I said. But more insulted the man persisted.

In the lavatory he squared his fists and approached me:
'Now you can talk.' I backed over cold stone in
A room that contained us and joined us. 'It's all so silly,'
I pleaded, searching for spaces to be alone in.

I shrank from his strangeness, not only afraid.
But at last of course I suffered what could not be delayed,
The innocuous struggle, the fighting words, 'bastard' and 'fuck',
A torn shirt and my lip numb and bloody,
My anger and - strange - the feel of my own body
New to me, as I struck, as he struck.

                    JAMES SIMMONS

Empty Raft

You tramped round the town
with half-baked notions
in your head of hunting down
finality in faces and stone buildings.

But nothing stood its ground.
Name-saked streets led
to blunt and bitter expressions -
everyone had blood on their hands.

The contract was exploited,
half-truths about 'a people'
who marched to the call
of imagination, all-in-all.

It was no good.
People and images were dead.

The natal relationship
was cracking at the seams,
unconscious it threw up
the truth, not dreams:

brutal, smashed ideals
like bits of glass
on the roadside.

Who bent down to ask
why he died
or her: any of us?

The process went wrong,
fouled-up, inadequate,
and you presumed
to create.
        A bit late
perhaps,
        no fairy tales left
to drift along on,
but a burnt-out
conclusion like
an empty raft.

        GERALD DAWE

Glass Grass
    'Understand that you yourself
    are guilty of every atrocity
    howsoever far from you
    it seems to be happening.'
        Günter Eich

The scorched cloth smell and smell of burnt flesh
From morning, a bomb in one of the parked cars,
The gulls, glinting like ice on asphalt in April,
The sun, in a smog of cheap petrol exhaust
Fumes: all bring on the sinusy migraine ...

Trudging against an east wind from the Cement
Factory ('awful bad for the chist!') - I wade
Through broken glass in a yellowing black smoke
Through steel-smouldering streets. There's broken glass
In my wedding shoes. (I wore them for luck!)

Ducking flying glass from the workers cleaning
Up afterwards, I take to the middle of Royal Avenue
On my way in gold rimmed polaroids to give
A poetry reading at Ballymurphy: clutching at
Ragged editions of my own poems, like clutching at

Strands of grass to hold you up from falling
With the crashing debris down the mountainy warehouses and hotels!. I promised John Hewitt and Des
Wilson, otherwise, I wouldn't venture forth again
Into this too near to the knuckle disaster ...

Tired of trying to pretend I am not this frightening
Freak has something in common with the terrorist
Of women and children, I read my poem about
The 'icons and the guns' and ask 'Now is
That 'sectarian?' '
            'We're all sectarian here!'

Some honest person replies. In the discussion after
-wards Des Wilson says 'I'm frightened of poets:
I'm frightened of their perceptions!' He wants me to answer
'Can you put yourself into the mind of the man who kills?'
'No!' I lie to the priest, 'I can't' but I can, I'm polluted

With the poison of violence, born and bred into it:
I'm dying of those dark looks I get from boy
Soldiers from slits in 'pigs' and I try to rub
The hatred from my eyes but it's deeper than 'looks':
The black is in my lungs now, and in my poems.

My fellow poets call my poems 'cryptic, crude, distasteful, brutal, savage, bitter ...' and I remember
The cobbles, cluttered from broken glass, glittered
Like hailstones melting in the warm May noon, and yet
I can put myself into the mind of the man who is cold,

The rich and reverend doctors who live off the misery
Of the people like leeches, the fat-faced politicians
Grinning on TV at their own witticisms, that all
I want to do is to lie down and join the other
Grinners, grinning with horror, the skull ones,

The 'ones who died' and who are about to die.
(O how did all this happen inside and behind time
And why so often?) I am on the same anti-
Depressant as the back street kids and their young mothers!
On the streets again, cluttered with broken glass,

White houses, charred black, dear God! Rosín
Somebody (arrested three times by the British Army
For giving her name in Irish) drives us back
Into black smoke. Is Violet Street on fire?
We cut down across from Brian's Mini Market

Through a Crocus Street maze to the Springfield Road.
The girl I saw on Earls Court Street does not
Matter in this Barracks Defense Mechanism
Spreading its virgin male cancer cells:
A black dog, erect, a tin in its teeth

Is running between foot-ball-kicking boys
Does not see the face-fallen girl cry
Nor care. A dog has more of an in, in our very
Own BOYS' WORLD ... A sudden black snow of
Charred newspapers, a lava of lead-pencil leaves:

The chimney-pots flowering smoke for tea time,
And Belfast is a beaten sexless dog, hushed,
Waiting for when or where the next blow
Will fall. Against this black, the white sea gulls
Glide in again, like hazy eyed drunks, over dark

Old ladies behind back yard walls, emptying slops ...
O old age 'prisoners' still watching your steps
Pray you for us 'bombs' in time-parked cars
By back-street pubs, about to burst
Into smithereens: 'fragments resulting from blows'.

PADRAIC FIACC

Belfast Street 1974

The glass glitters in the gutter.
Fragments heap up like hail.
Sharp flints and flakes are jammed
In window corners,
Between flagstones.

Each is a shard only,
Torn from its proper use,
Condemned to death
Surely as autumn leaf,
Though unlike leaf, it gives
No nutriment to earth.

META MAYNE REID

Dull Spring Cantata
for Geraldine in Italy

Across the water plains
    a wind shoves mist
into mist, fog into mystery,
    that rasps in the chest
    and slurs the hours.

Wrought in tar and wood
and suffering the vice of hardship
and the scream of paper gulls
over the shipyard waste,
    and the clouds scratching
the ridges of the concrete,
    the 'town' settles
    beneath the 'hill'
    like running lead.

Finger-swept doors in
    every house,
fingers in every eye;
Belfast or Berlin,
they prize the same sky
    but different walls ...

DENNIS KELLY

Across the Water

Across the water
the white geese and the black
pecking each other
merge into grey.

Night falls.
Beneath the skull
moon the Minotaur
blind and frenzied
in his Labyrinth is demagogue
and king
and Christ the king of kings.

Each dawn, the blood
is swallowed by the sea.
Night and day and night
merge into grey.

MAOL MACMULLEN

Floods

At high tide the sea is under the city,
A natural subversive, the Farset,
Forced underground, observes no curfew,
And, sleepless in their beds, the sullen drains
Move under manholes.

Blame falls on the builders, foolish men.
The strained civility of city, sea, breaks
Yearly, snapped by native rains,
Leaving in low streets the sandbagged doors,
The furnished pavements.

FRANK ORMSBY

Belfast Teenager 1974

God no, please!
give me violence
again, to drown this silence
which is killing me.

... big streets empty, full of little
papers, cigarette ends, decaying spittle
and walking here causes only the dust
to move.

Where are the noises then? Talking,
laughing, coughing, spitting, walking
around these no-people streets, and
where are the bloody people?

It looks as if the city
has been taken over by pretty
flowers, big churches and
their always erect steeples.
Of course, there are soldiers
roaring past in empty roads.
I might be the last person here,
and only nothing to fear.

The people, all in their houses
frightened of going out to places:
stay with John Wayne and keep
        their faces
for the windows.

The big wind blows
all the dust to other footpaths,
nice and empty ...

The snobbie sun thinks he knows
it all, looking down, and he can only see
someone spitting here.

It's only me!

                      P P

Fourth Movement: Epilogues

For Tom and Ann, Leaving

The Right to Work,
'March for the Right to Work'
And two hundred out of
Ten Thousand
Lined up
With their Lunch Boxes;

Romantic Ireland's dead and gone
Its eggs, tomatoes, bolts
And two fingers from the women
And a telephoto lens
(for future reference)
From the men;

They claimed their Supplementary
While you marched
Then emigrated two weeks later,
After the nods and nudges
And the mock machine gun rattles
Isolated you at work;

There was 'No Intimidation'
Just men - hung back
When you left the yard
'Bullets can spread'
They told you 'in a joke';

Romantic Ireland's
Dead and gone
And there's more than
O'Leary in the grave.

                 MICHAEL BROPHY

Icon
for my brother, Peter, serving in the Alps

Unholy Mother Ireland banging
On the wall in labour

Each season believed
Ivy and thorn could flower

Fell
    slumped over
The Sewing Machine

'Christ of Almighty' swore
Down through a childhood
       only
A woman or child could bear

Left each one of us with
A grave grace, dark

Not just the same thing as
Wisdom, that what

A *Terribilità* frowning
Nefertiti brow

Vowed never to
Scratch a grey hair
And now, indeed, did not

We were born in her

Screams to 'Get Out!'

                    PADRAIC FIACC

Emigrants, Refugees

Smallchurch an aquarium of air,
Lungs labouring the supply
Under spinning blades of sycamore.
Hyphenated coughs heave and settle;
Eclipsing sounds rebound
To ease an absence:

Then the priest appears,
Movements cut and clinical.

Emigrants, refugees, shuffle upright;
Strong faces set to make God matter,
These have held to the bells ringing:
Left digs, converged upon their
    upbringing
Prayer seems to make the air mosaic,
I think about the Pearl of great price,
A pebble of energy in the mind's lake;
And concentric thoughts rippling
In a two thousand year old wake.

Mass ended: the Everlasting
    Arms release
Doors open altarwise:
Into spectrum heart high May.
With them, I feel the depths of
    centuries -
A mountain gully; some shaggy glen.
Tonight I'll keep in touch by screen:
Mountains and roots will ride a
    pale blue ray.

                  BRENDAN HAMILL

Keeping My Place

1

In fortunate places
They worry only
About a prospect of rain -
Who's for tennis
Deckchairs parasols
Shopping without
Barriers soldiers saracens
The person touched by strangers
War conditions with
The enemy inside:
What private hate
Wrecked the Abercorn;
What faceless lout
Gutted Smithfield?

In a wet jilting June
I review and assess
What I have made of half
A century and guess
With trepidation what
I'll do with a handful of years
A post-dated cheque
To be marked invalid perhaps
By a bankrupt bank:

2

I began in violence and
My age now coincides
With hooded murder and
My children know no other
Place or style
Than the bomb the fist and thugs'
Intimidation
The tortured corpse in the ditch:

3

The toad puffs the snake smiles
Cancelled faces kill -
I recall two figures poised
Between the sea and the shore
On the fringe of life
In my early fatherhood;
Yes they
Had the luck to be gay
Or to be nonchalant
To whom I sang old songs
Driving the car
Through strange townlands:

4

The toad bellows and the snake snarls.
Father greying the younger ones
Have seldom grasped
Bucket and spade with blood
Coursing like sea
From the Irish curse that wrecked
Picnics and destinations -
(Yeats and Mitchel too:
War in our time O Lord)
May peace and peace and peace
Be everywhere:

5

I declare
That in this vicious town
Where the future hangs
Like washing on a line
Depending on weather
Anonymous masked men
Cudgel petrol bomb:
That along High Street
A river used to stride
Sails in the air
A semaphore

Now stammering underground
So that I stop and look
At the trees my father made;
Stumbling I look around
At the loss and the waste
Enormous desolation:
Myself my poetry and soon
My children stooping to lick
And stick down emigrants' labels.

      ROY McFADDEN

Emigrant Brother

They said you would be back soon
But it is seven years now
Since I stood childishly choked
At the Heysham boat
Spilling through my eyes goodbye.
Remember Saturday morning pillow-fights
And headstones in the sun
Seen through dimpled glass
Of our small box room window.

London drank you in like a new beer
To tube trains towing fog in winter
And kites, like pet hawks riding high
Over Hampstead Heath in summer.
This summer, strangers for a year
We'll drink in Highgate Village.
They said you would be back soon
But you asked 'What for?'

      BRENDAN HAMILL

An Ulster Garland

Close by my kitchen window juts
a wall, rich-textured, scarred
brickwork of ochre, grey and red
many times cemented, showing
faint whitewash from before
the house was last patched up.
And where the roof of split slates slopes
to its corner has somehow taken
root among fissures a sprig
of wallflowers, arching
luminous now in the late sunshine.

Delicate, the flowers
have survived nights, and many downpours,
found sustenance amid crumbling.
I have come to expect them.

No, they would not, should it come,
prevail against bulldozer, or bomb;
nor admit their relevance.
And should these petals be torn by explosion,
buried deep under rubble, so
each unique thing must be lost, and is
irrevocable; yet always

others continue, reappear
contriving such root somewhere, so
configured on moving skies.

I drop my gaze on close
unfocused roofline ridges set
at jarring angles.
            This
is Ireland now, where mobs command
and kill, and terror grips.
'The power system is at breakdown point.'

Lightless, I look
again for the yellow flowers upon
their brink; also remark
among the streets' cross-hatching sprays
of answering greenery, deepening
as day ebbs; in low
untended yards, how cranesbill, vetch,
sweetrocket, speedwell, flowers

run wild I have no name for,
sustain their points of colour; and grass
persists, unorganised. By kind
pervasive to outlast
what coming darkness.

ANDREW WATERMAN

Before Salamis

The Persian galleys plumed with warriors
move, dolphin-curved, across the ivory sea.
Flutes set a speed for oars. King Xerxes broods
above the bay and prays to barbaric gods.

Greece stirred at dawn. At sunrise raised shields gleamed
and trumpet-calls set all the caves and cliffs
ablaze with sound.
        And up Cithaeron's roads
in lonely farmsteads mothers caught the cry -
faint as a serpent's hiss, and horrible -
and clasped their children in the shadowy rooms.

W B STANFORD

Edvard Munch

You would think with so much going on outside
The deal table would make for the window,
The ranged crockery freak and wail
Remembering its dark origins, the frail
Oilcloth, in a fury of recognitions,
Disperse in a thousand directions,
And the simple bulb in the ceiling, honed
By death to a worm of pain, to a hair
Of heat, to light snowflake laid
In a dark river at night (and wearied
Above all by the life-price of time
And the failure by only a few tenths
Of an inch but completely and for ever
Of the ends of a carefully drawn equator
To meet, sing and be one) abruptly
Roar into the floor.
        But it
Never happens like that. Instead

There is this quivering silence
In which, day by day, the play
Of light and shadow (shadow mostly)
Repeats itself, though never exactly.

This is the all-purpose bed-, work- and bedroom.
Its mourning faces are cracked porcelain only quicker,
Its knuckles doorknobs only lighter,
Its occasional cries of despair
A function of the furniture.

        DEREK MAHON

No Ivory Tower

I do not envy those
who write in locked studies,
in Ivory Towers.
Give me the rub of circumstance,
the electricity which springs
from daily living.
I will not,
like puss in the midnight dark,
stalk my prey in a shuttered room,
will not entreat
honourable words to visit humble pages,
as I sit, insulated by silence.

I will write at the bus stop,
in the kitchen, between form-filling.
If my thoughts refuse
to clamour for words' clothing
let them die naked.
They must pierce through life
as infant's thrusting head
breaks the womb's waters,
before I will give them names,
and own them as my children.

      META MAYNE REID

Under a Cloud

Nothing was more under a cloud than a tempting prospect,
yet the poets would keep expectation above the dead level,

Hamlets for whom the end would be achieved
not with murder but the opposite of murder.
They were present as an unknown quality,
to control facile expectancy, stir non-urgent
    wishes, unsafe proposals.
Did they expect the Prime Minister on a balcony
    to announce some slight utopia?
Or should the poets themselves, legislatively,
    offer a dream?

                        GEORGE BUCHANAN

Fitts

Paleface mirrored in the window grime,
how you practise to dissemble.
These preying eyes, this mouth mad
to eat the city, pull them your lover
face, show us your cavities and
smile and smile and be a villain.
You're a house buzzing with glory holes.
You're a badge of all you've kissed and told,
you're the lovely man, a cast of millions.
Try and pull us your death mask. Try and
ingratiate yourself with soil.

A lady that was brisk and bold
came riding o'er the fermie brae,
a firehaired woman, who gave him his red
letter-day. She made him glory in
his sad dishabells, in his glad rags.
She cancelled all of his dead letters;
and all the next day his sense clothed
in her salvation garments; hands
gloved in her dark musk, mouth
tender with her mouth, tongue
poignant with her breath, the coat
of her body cleaving to him as
he walks the street in all his canker.

Will you look at yon poetry man.
Hey, fatstock, Hopalong.
Give us a snatch of your clownish song.
He wants to shimmy rings round you.
He wants the world to love him to death.
He thinks that he's the man in the street

and that's who the streets belong to. Ask him
what side he's on, he'll tell you
the people's side - that's all the sides.
He wonders whether the next split
gutbag might be his own, maybe.
He's frightened his words'll be stubbed out.
But he belly laughs. He's not wise.

       STEWART PARKER

The Singing Lady

We saw her in Linenhall Street
Behind the BBC
A small lady
In suit of sober tweed

And she was alone and singing
On that August sunday evening
When the light was failing
And her voice was high and trembling.

Just look at that
Said my female friend
What ever is it
Some sort of nut?

That is a singing lady I said
Singing in suit of tweed
With a tweed hat on her head
Singing psalm ninety-eight

Second version to the tune Stuttgart,
She is not nuts

She is a single lady transmitter
Her audience is her Creator
And those that pass her
Can you think of a better

Thing to do behind the BBC
In Linenhall Street
At nine-thirty
pm on an August sunday?

       TOM MATTHEWS

The Nightowl

The nightowl preys
the breadth of the moon,
confronts the crossfire
between the men above
and the men below.

The nightowl escapes
to the dark side.
I will not pursue him
or bring him down to earth.
For me his secrets soar.

           WILLIAM PESKETT

Business it Seems is Still Business

What they say about the lyric poet
is not true.
I have seen him at close range and I know it
for a lie -
How beautifully marked he is by life!
How gay and generous of heart!
How easily made cry!

Sweet Christ! is that what they would like us to believe?
When like a fool, I slobbered on my sleeve
And croaked out love, he was the one
Who understood it all, the soothing tongue
Saying, 'love's our crime and lovers much abused.'
And when my sobbing settled for a time
His little mind applied itself to rhyme
To see what it could lift to the sublime
And how this latest crisis could be used.

           TOM McLAUGHLIN

A Fable
for Tom Kilroy

To take an unmeasured leap
From a ladder through a lobe
Of glass and still get shot
As a house-painter did

Recently in Belfast,
Is perhaps a form of flight
That I would, were I able,
Offer you as a fable.
But it is in fighting
Out such images that infer
Fate is unable to err

In its aim even once
Among the long blades of glass
That leap for the surrendered
Body in their high
Instantaneous chimes,
That I am writing
Out this report
Of the incident. There is
A question of fate
To be considered, but only
After the stricter question

Of hate, who fired the gun?
And why should the fable
Not act in curt accord
With the fact? To fall
Through the surrounding glass
And to have the delicate
Ear-bones taken away
By a bullet, to feel fear,
Run, become the stricken deer,
Is an available form of defeat
We have too easily learned.

Look at the place, at the young
Gunman. Face his face.
Forget the brilliance of flight,
Admit the kudos he earned
for having killed a Teague,
Feel the feeling he learned
At that unfeeling age.
Don't think of them as Fate
Taking its toll of the race,
Don't try to be doubly kind
To killer and killed.

If all hold it in mind
That killers will be killed, that
The clear-sighted see the blind

Inscrutable face of Fate
Swarming with acne
And adolescent hate, then all should find
True reason for despair
In the story. There is ground
For this when we believe
Fate seeks the pursued.
True, but even truer,

With the pursuer, Fate is found.
I can imagine unmeasured
Glass and the great rivers
It runs into when a man
Bursts storming through its skin.
But I can also imagine
His head, bloodied, and the bullet
Lodged in thunder within;
And the chance that tomorrow
The killer will hear glass bells
Breaking; and that Fate

Has nothing to do with him.
This is my point in writing. Writing
Not the admiration of fighting
Or flight, which is for many;
But the desire to be no fewer
Than both pursued and pursuer.
Whatever image you lob
Someone comes on still holding
A gun. He has to be got,
That unfinished youth who fires the shot.
I write to finish the job.

SEAMUS DEANE

Letter to Seamus Heaney

From Carrigskeewaun in Killadoon
I write, although I'll see you soon,
Hoping this fortnight detonates
Your year in the United States,
Offering you by way of welcome
To the sick counties we call home
The mystical point at which I tire
Of Calor gas and a turf fire.

Till we talk again in Belfast
Pleasanter far to leave the past
Across three acres and two brooks
On holiday in a post box
Which dripping fuchsia bells surround,
Its back to the prevailing wind,
And where sanderlings from Iceland
Court the breakers, take my stand,

Disinfecting with a purer air
That small subconscious cottage where
The Irish poet slams his door
On slow-worm, toad and adder:
Beneath these racing skies it is
A tempting stance indeed - *ipsis
Hibernicis hiberniores* -
Except that we know the old stories,

The midden of cracked hurley sticks
Tied to recall the crucifix,
Of broken bones and lost scruples,
The blackened hearth, the blazing gable's
Telltale cinder where we may
Scorch our shins until that day
We sleepwalk through a No Man's Land
Lipreading to an Orange band.

Continually, therefore, we rehearse
Goodbyes to all our characters
And, since both would have it both ways,
On the oily roll of calmer seas
Launch coffin-ship and life-boat,
Body with soul thus kept afloat,
Mind open like a half-door
To the speckled hill, the plovers' shore.

So let it be the lapwing's cry
That lodges in the throat as I
Raise its alarum from the mud,
Seeking for your sake to conclude
Ulster Poet our Union Title
And prolong this sad recital
By leaving careful footprints round
A wind-encircled burial mound.

MICHAEL LONGLEY

Tribute to a Reporter in Belfast

Poets, is not this solitary man's own
    uniquely
utilitarian technique of truth-telling
this finely apparent effort of his
to split the atom of a noun and reach truth
    through language,
to chip-carve each word and report
as if language itself were the very
    conscience of reality -
a poetry more
than poetry is.
Tonight once more he has done his work
    with words
and fish roots and echoes of all manner
    and kind
did flower up out of an ocean-floor
    resonance
so rapidly but with such clarity
that you were made to look out of the eyes
    of another
even as the other shot you dead in the back,
out of the eyes of a catholic republican
whose grandparents were quakers in
    Norwich,
but likewise out of the eyes
of a seventeenth-century Norfolkman in
    Virginia
sailing a copper knife through the soft
    pink air
of an Indian's open mouth ...

Gratias for the verbal honesty of Liam
    Hourican
in a country where words also have died an
    unnatural death
or else have been used on all sides for
    unnatural ends
and by poets as much as by gunmen or
    churchmen.
Day and night his integrity of words has
    sustained us.

                        PAUL DURCAN

Rage for Order

Somewhere beyond
The scorched gable end
And the burnt-out
Buses there is a poet indulging his
Wretched rage for order -

Or not as the
Case may be, for his
Is a dying art,
An eddy of semantic scruple
In an unstructurable sea.

He is far
From his people,
And the fitful glare
Of his high window is as
Nothing to our scattered glass.

His posture is
Grandiloquent and
Deprecating, like this,
His diet ashes,
His talk of justice and his mother

The rhetorical
Device of a Claudian emperor -
Nero if you prefer,
No mother there;
And this in the face of love, death and the wages of the poor.

If he is silent ·
It is the silence
Of enforced humility,
If anxious to be heard
It is the anxiety of a last word

When the drums start -
For this is a dying art.
Now watch me
As I make history,
Watch as I tear down

To build up
With a desperate love,
Knowing it cannot be

Long now till I have need of his
Germinal ironies.

DEREK MAHON

Ways of Failing

Modes of expression pass.
We are born into tradition,
Acknowledge masters no more
Harmful than wine tasters,
Whose cellars, small but chosen
Of the best, become the best.

But soils change. The worm
Turns and dies. The wood
May hold the wine for more
Or less one generation,
But no more. With care
We learn of better and best.

Words are not wine: at best
They taste of the man, the year,
The state of the soil, the hail
Beating or sun sleeping
Over the harvest; more
At best can be inferred,

Tradition, labour, care
Expended elsewhere to make
An appropriate gift or a way
Of making amends; but whatever
We do for pleasure is done
According to rules of its own.

To rules that alter with what
We are trying to say, reflecting
Ways of failing and failing
Or seeming to fail, the more
Or less honest phrase dividing
The better and best effect -
Which remains when emotion passes,
When modes of expression pass.

ANDREW WHITTAKER

Poets Today

Poets today
Are silent as the grave.
Or to put it another way:
Poets today
Are gravely silent.

Poets, they say
(In a roundabout way)
In this or any other age
Being poets
Should mind their ways.

Being political, they say
Is not poetical,
Neither is it practical
And does not rhyme
At this time.

The question is
How best to stand aside
To look as if
You hadn't died
Were not mouldering

Fading
Disappearing
Into
Thin
Air

Where it's always difficult to hear -
Gunfire.

PATRICK GALVIN

Ulster Today
for John Montague

Sitting at my desk among papers
I wonder nothing that troubles the TV News
moves me to write. The tragedy and the betrayals:
an honest busdriver shot, a soldier
kicking a mouthing intellectual,
an exploded pub, boys throwing stones

that must hurt, running towards the camera,
grinning. I have nothing to add:
the stones hurt, the smiling boys are boys
the farcical and painful history of Ireland
is with us, unchanged. If the next bomb
kills *me* it will still be irrelevant.
If the next soldier kicks me - by mistake -
it will only be sore.
    Whereas
the silly reviews in the *Irish Times*
have driven me mad! If I could only find
last night's edition I'd show them where I stand.

          JAMES SIMMONS

An Urgent Letter
for James Simmons

So this is, Jimmy, where we live;
And Ulster is the name you give
to home as to Belfast, Bogside,
all the streets where men have died.
Here in a corner of the cave
the beasts are quiet who are alive.

We both agree on this - to ditch
all who call the place a bitch
for easy money in magazines,
or rhyme a cheque-book lodged in pain.
The blood-banks never had our trade;
our tribal credits are unpaid.

Your boat's at bay, your kids at home;
you write of summers yet to come;
the wind is full of condiments
as verse is of commonsense.
But if I try to call it salt
I suspect that you will fault

my sophistry that puts a name
on two things which are the same;
reply, my mind is puritan
and even my drink god-ridden -
HEDLEY MURPHY GOSPELPREACHER
on tea-bags of our local grocer,

But pardon me; I find these parts
keen to perfect our passive arts.
The girls I meet with were wide
in the tail and bushy-eyed,
while men in pubs sit on wishing
instead of just-a-fishing.

These are heroes? Just like Brecht
who proved that freedom is neglect?
What of the guns that we have seen
in a shop-window in Coleraine
for sale between the hooks and bait,
the bandoliers and the long-range sights?

And hell lies near us. Look and see
our gods are changed to infantry.
The ancient saracens now lurch
protectively around your church;
the infamous blood-and-water gash
is swaddled under an orange sash.

I too deplore the patent Muse
would make our every line a fuse.
But winters follow when the banks
approach new customers in tanks
and better men that we are sink
riddled with something worse than drink.

And fuses are designed to fail,
to drop the overloaded tale,
too great a shock. Thicker cable
tolerates the current fable
with tonic hum and decorum
giving death its silent quorum.

We both approve of bridge and sex,
prefer this world to the next.
So by the summer we'll forget
the bitter words I may have said.
But please remember, if you will,
there is little time left to kill.

Derry 1973

HUGH MAXTON

The Night Air

The night-air knows us, follows
the long line of our bodies, flowing
across us and down

in the street now, I look too hard
and too suddenly at strangers
and they are disconcerted as one
is disconcerted by a cripple

the night-air knows us, follows
the long line of our bodies, does not
distinguish between us.

GEOFFREY SQUIRES

That Stranger

A stranger from the past reveals
where you are failing and where you lie.
She undresses and begins to point
where the battles were fought where the battles were won.
And inside yourself you notice an army moving still.

PAUL YATES

Sheepman

Even the barflies move to corner tables,
Mouthing 'Sheepman'. The barman serves,
But grudgingly. Like Mexicans and half-
Breeds I must wear that special hangdog look,
Say nothing.

There is too much cattle country. The range
Is free in theory, cowmen find
Excuses to resent the different.
They say that cows won't feed where sheep have fed.
Pathetic.

Don't say the outcast has his dignity.
Perhaps it's something not to thrive
On brawn, or trample those whose small stampedes

Hurt no-one; such victories are thin, cold
Consolation.

Not cowed I claim my rights - to herd alone.
And be accepted. When I skirt
The rim of cattle drives, salute me,
And when I come to share your bunkhouse fire,
Make room.

        FRANK ORMSBY

Parting

How strange we are sitting here
In a waiting-room full of strangers -
Our parting unwitnessed, as those dreams
We summoned once disperse themselves to
An oblivion, like the smoke swirling
To the station-rafters outside.

'God, I was so wrong about you.'
There is such beauty in the profile
Your composure allows my wounded gaze,
Such promising warmth in your ice-cold grasp.
And all I can do is whine sorrow,
Paving any reluctance in you with certainty.

That you are going I must accept.
And still I try kindling the ashes, with
The clock breathing heavily on the wall -
Its panting now filling your ears
Disturbing you, drawing you from unheard words
Down an exclusive time-table, to your passing.

        MICHAEL McGINLEY

Song for Sinn Fein for Serena

The beach.
On.
Ourselves alone are walking
With songs
(Song: an interpretation of the beach)
On smooth sand, shallow pools
Windows of water in

Kelly shovel and empty tin of beans for
Sandworms.

(Interpretation: an imagination of the beach)
New like the sand of the moon
And maybe the new airletter from there a song
Idealism has a hole in it and whoops we go
Through it to a beach
That never existed.
Ourselves alone
Like hermits going in
Going out of water and sand
Beach so lonesome we died and walked
Out on it.

JAMES LIDDY

The Indians on Alcatraz

Through time their sharp features
Have softened and blurred,
As if they still inhabited
The middle distances,
As if these people have never
Stopped riding hard

In an opposite direction,
The people of the shattered lances
Who have seemed forever going back.
To have willed this reservation,
It is as if they are decided
To be islanders at heart,

As if this island
Has forever been the destination
Of all those dwindling bands.
After the newspaper and TV reports
I want to be glad that
Young Man Afraid Of His Horses Lives

As a brilliant guerrilla fighter,
The weight of his torque
Worn like the moon's last quarter,
Though only if he believes
As I believed of his fathers,
That they would not attack after dark.

PAUL MULDOON

Downpatrick Mental Hospital

The grounds are very neatly kept.
Here they cut his legs off
bit by bit. Gangrene
in his toes first
then his shins and thighs
crept with monstrous and triumphant
prudery towards his gulled genitals.

They gave him salt baths while he whimpered.

They let me in and out
of that strong hygienic place,
unlocking doors and locking them behind me.
He had me to visit him - the rest
are zealously forgotten
where Patrick put down
bloody Celtic practices
and cast out the old gods,
calling them devils.

      MAOL MACMULLEN

Getting Home

In the ward's white and blue
Nursery shades that pen the slobbering old,
We found you, arranged for us in a chair:
Mother sat still, love bare.
My gummy-eyed aunt fed you sticky sweets,
Wanting I think - as the truely dull do -
To drag gentle craziness back to sense.
I leaned into your childish talk, prattled
Childishly with you, laughed, and all the time
Hurt in our house of grown, sharpened words.

Father, you were young at sixty. I
Was your awkward only boy, dumbly
Asking a way to walk. Soon enough
A cloud of our ill blood had kissed your brain,
I had walked from a small town's denial,
My clenched home, the sick place where you were -

But when the summer funeral of dark-
Suited men carried you I was among

Nursery shades of speaking, small, alone,
Suddenly un-named in the bigger town,
Wanting to walk with you through our town ...

When I stood at your grave
I heard the bells of the dust
Toll my name to the town's root.

I saw the lock and dark on home undone,
Our name in stone a child's direction on,
Your dark, a door to the sun.

In the earth you were
Like wind like fire like rain
Calling:

I was everywhere, answering.

PATRICK WILLIAMS

The Field Hospital

Taking, giving back their lives
By the strength of our bare hands,
By the silence of our knives,
We answer to no grey South

Nor blue North, nor self defence,
The lie of just wars, neither
Cold nor hot blood's difference
In their discharging of guns,

But that hillside of fresh graves.
Would this girl brought to our tents
From whose flesh we have removed
Shot that George, on his day off,

Will use to weight fishing lines,
Who died screaming for ether,
Yet protest our innocence?
George lit the lanterns, in danced

Those gigantic, yellow moths
That brushed right over her wounds,
Pinning themselves to our sleeves
Like medals given the brave.

PAUL MULDOON

Downpatrick

1

The houses in Irish Street
Cling like clegs
And English Street
Steeples up to three
Saints on the cathedral;
But Scotch Street slopes
Away from the river
The swans and the island:
The Welsh I suppose
Given Saint Patrick
Declined to reside
By river or steeple.

2

My father was born there
In a brisk town, then the Quoile
Familiar with barges before
The railway came and Belfast
Killed crafts - Quoile furniture -
(Lynn Doyle on the wireless; Irish Chippendale).
But the swans remained on the river
Icebergs or islands
A wish of water away
From the steam, the steel and the hammer.

3

The swans I remember and
The cathedral footed
And feted with April daffodils
Glimpsed from the fretting train then
When exhausted with refugees
From German bombs it stumbled forward
To a future of Irish bombs uniting
The grief of a girl
With one eye and an arm.

ROY McFADDEN

from Clinical Notes
'Ieti discrimina parva'

A staff nurse through the sleeping ward
Rustles like a sigh. Tonight my mind
Runs calm and clear: runs all on you,
Old friend, lonely in your distant glen
And vilified by your own kind.
What comfort can I give you then?
I picture you, beside a great turf fire
Reading late or dozing in your chair
While the North Atlantic gasps outside
And gripes through its black gullet from Kintyre
To Benmore Head.
                You knew the cost
Of not stampeding with the rest
Or hurling a bomb or abuse
Was ostracism at the best -
At worst, a bullet in the back,
But 'Charity comes first,' you said
'Not justice. Justice without charity
Will never reconcile or make us whole.'
Well, those words were mouthed into the gale
And torn away. Against such odds
As faced you for a lifetime none
But a fool would so persist, or one of God's
Own saints - only to see the politics
Of outrage and atrocity prevail,
Mere Yahoos trample down the State,
Wreck at random, maim and kill:
Worse, cripple minds and mutilate the will.

I've no comfort, then, for you,
Only reasons for despair. Besides,
What's left for you or me to do -
So brittle are the fictions now
That shield us from death's truth - except
To write our memoirs while we may?
'My God, no, Not yet,' you'll say.
'For after charity come faith and hope,
Not self-justification. And anyway,
I've no choice. The work goes on because it must,
And will, long after I am dust.'

I'm not so sure; and yet it comforts me
This pitching night flecked by the spume

And slobber of the maniacal sea
To know the candle shines still in your room.

NORMAN DUGDALE

One Day in August

One day in August, going by bus to Annalong,
Past fields brown-pimpled with haycocks,
And whitewashed rectangular houses,
I tried - expatriate now - to overhear
The homely rhythms that these people use
As running murmurs to a simple way of life.
Through their world's wilderness of tangled hate
I tried to see the obverse of the coins
That tinkle brash in every little till
And echo that intolerance I know too well.
Then came that answer on that August day:
If you would find the virtue of this place
Then search it out in tidy village streets
And in the narrow, stone-walled fields,
For there these people build in quietness,
Far from the bigot's drumming rant
That tears the fabric of this land.

ROBERT GREACEN

'These People'

It's not 'These People'
Way out there.

We are the People
Here and now
And we are

The People who
Have the finger

On the trigger.

JOE CAMPLISSON

Neither an Elegy nor a Manifesto
for the people of my province and the rest of Ireland

Bear in mind these dead:
I can find no plainer words.
I dare not risk using
that loaded word, Remember,
for your memory is a cruel web
threaded from thorn to thorn across
a hedge of dead bramble, heavy
with pathetic atomies.

I cannot urge or beg you
to pray for anyone or anything,
for prayer in this green island
is tarnished with stale breath,
worn smooth and characterless
as an old flagstone, trafficked
with journeys no longer credible
to lost destinations.

The careful words of my injunctions
are unrhetorical, as neutral
and unaligned as any I know:
they propose no more than thoughtful response;
they do not pound with the drum-beats
of patriotism, loyalty, martyrdom.

So, I say only: Bear in mind
these men and lads killed in the streets,
but do not differentiate between
those deliberately gunned-down
and those caught by unaddressed bullets:
such distinctions are not relevant.

Bear in mind the skipping child hit
by the anonymous ricochet;
the man shot at his own fireside
with his staring family round him;
the elderly Salvationist wife
making tea for the firemen
when the wall collapsed;
and the garrulous neighbours at the bar
when the bomb exploded near them;
the gesticulating deaf-mute stilled
by the soldier's rifle in the town square;

and the policeman dismembered
by the booby-trap in the car.

I could have made a lilting gazetteer,
cadenced like a ballad or a folk-song,
of the place-names where these several deaths occurred:
but if we are always to continue dancing
through the same stencilled rhythms,
there will be new names, surely, and
the old names will carry
new cargoes of grief.

I might have recited a pitiful litany
of the names of all the dead:
but these could effectively be presented
only in small batches,
like a lettered tablet in a village church,
valid while everyone knew everyone,
or longer, where family names persist.

Accident, misfortune, disease, coincidence
of genetic factors or social circumstance,
may summon courage, resolution, sympathy,
to whatever level one is engaged.
Natural disasters of lava and hurricane,
famine or flood in far countries, will evoke
compassion for the thin-shanked survivors.

Patriotism has to do with keeping
the country in good heart, the community
ordered with justice and mercy:
these will enlist loyalty and courage often,
and sacrifice, sometimes even martyrdom,
Bear these eventualities in mind also;
they will concern you forever:
but, at this moment, bear in mind these dead.

JOHN HEWITT

Lars

What need have you to ring the bell
Backwards in a muffled peal
Of mourning or regret? The small gods
Whom you serve - those deities
Of hearth and store - have served you well

Through garnered years. Upon your coasts
No storm-cones fly. Under a kindly sun
Among your spread of golden corn poppies
This autumn splash vermilion.

Considering the strata lie
Tilted north, how mean the soil, and thin
And bitter still the wind, no wonder that
My tillage here is slow to fructify,
Stubborn in its yield. Yet not this
Want of metamorphosis
Grieves me now. It might have plagued me once,
God knows. But not these mornings when,
A step beyond the door, feet slither in

Night-blood congealing on the stones.

NORMAN DUGDALE

In Kilroot, Co Antrim in Search of Swift

Under a grey sky, in the ruined church,
We stood among the dead crows, disappointed:
Was it a sheep-pen, pig-sty or cow-shed?
We watched for a minute, but awe was out of place
Beside this smell of death and dung.
Then we thought it was a careless world
And plagues to great men meant respect;
But farmers here keep pigs, and crows are pests.
From his grave the Mad Dean would agree:
No culture-vulutres dare to trespass here!

JACK HOLLAND

Provincial Down

The shadows-produce of a low, full sun
On a low graph line of hills where
Orchards career apples like eyes
The globes of earth blown life-size on their trees
The diving rods of car lamps unearth
At nights a way ahead
Through towns the shape and size
A boyhood's spent in, their buildings
Meant in an age to be walked

Or slow horse-drawn past. Their men,
An accent that must penetrate
Even to its singing voice, not knowing
The final shape of Africa
Not showing in their eyes, scrimp shelter
Under six-inch lintel'd doorways, small
Hot turds of ash forming
At the ends of their belittled cigarettes.
An awkward wind -
That rinds would cherish oranges against.
Awkward as a woman throwing plates or stones,
Seems searching space for lost chaff.
             Some trees around
Some bear a plaque ('Know the Lord') nailed
Seven feet above the ground.
It's a slogan won't identify
Whose patch I wander on.

                                    LIAM LYNCH

Please Identify Yourself

British, more or less; Anglican, of a kind.
In Cookstown I dodge the less urgent question
when a friendly Ulsterbus driver raises it;
'You're not a Moneymore girl yourself?' he asks,
deadpan. I make a cowardly retrogression,
slip ten years back. 'No, I'm from New Zealand.'
'Are you now? Well, that's a coincidence:
the priest at Moneymore's a New Zealander.'
And there's the second question, unspoken.
Unanswered.
            I go to Moneymore
anonymously, and stare at all three churches.

In Belfast, though, where sides have to be taken,
I stop compromising - not that you'd guess,
seeing me hatless there among the hatted,
neutral voyeur among the shining faces
in the glossy Martyrs' Memorial Free Church,
The man himself is cheerleader in the pulpit
for crusader choruses; we're laved in blood,
marshalled in ranks. I chant the nursery tunes
and mentally cross myself. You can't stir me
with evangelistic hymns, Dr Paisley:
I know them. Nor with your computer-planned

sermon - Babylon, Revelation, whispers
of popery, slams at the IRA, more blood.
I scrawl incredulous notes under my hymnbook
and burn with Catholicism.
              Later
hacking along the Lower Falls Road
against a gale, in my clerical black coat,
I meet a bright gust of tinselly children
in beads and lipstick and their mothers' dresses
for Hallowe'en; who chatter and surround me.
Overreacting once again (a custom
of the country, not mine alone) I give them
all my loose change for their rattling tin
and my blessing - little enough. But now
to my tough Presbyterian ancestors,
Brooks and Hamilton, lying in the graves
I couldn't find at Moneymore and Cookstown
among so many unlabelled bones, I say:
I embrace you also, my dears.

                        FLEUR ADCOCK

March

Stoned cheek turned again
The stone turned from the tomb:
Unvault spring
Like a lad
For your parish needs hoeing
And a weeding of snakes
In constricted land -

Because the houses are aghast
Mothers and children stay
Tears for another day
Since a corpse provided
Everyday:

Hold up your favour Patrick
Not like a riot shield
Or clerics with their bibles
But clear as clover clean
The guttering blood from the tarmac
Vengeance from old sick walls:

From Downpatrick Cathedral
(Abashed by daffodils)
Pronounce a curse on snakes
Fused to ejaculate -

From Downpatrick Cathedral
(Three saints smudged on a wall)
Now that Easter flusters
From the shattered egg
Stained window-glass and rubble
Chance another spring
With hailstones maybe
Or perhaps daffodils.

            ROY McFADDEN

The Bullaun

'Drink watèr from the hollow in the stone ...'
This was it, then - the cure for madness:
A rock with two round cavities, filled with rain;
A thing I'd read about once, and needed, then,
But since forgotten. I didn't expect it here -
Not having read the guidebook;
Not having planned, even, to be in Antrim.
'There's a round tower, isn't there?' I'd asked.
The friendly woman in the post office
Gave me directions: 'Up there past the station,
Keep left, on a way further - it's a fair bit -
And have you been to Lough Neagh yet?' I walked -
It wasn't more than a mile - to the stone phallus
Rising above its fuzz of beech-trees
In the municipal gardens. And beside it,
This. I circled around them,
Backing away over wet grass and beechmast,
Aiming the camera (since I had it with me,
Since I was playing tourist this afternoon)
And saw two little boys pelting across.
'Take our photo! Take our photo! Please!'
We talked it over for a bit -
How I couldn't produce one then and there;
But could I send it to them with the postman?
Well, could they give me their addresses?
Kevin Tierney and Declan McCallion,
Tobergill Gardens, I wrote, they stood and smiled,
I clicked, and waved goodbye, and went.

Two miles away, an hour later,
Heading dutifully through the damp golf-course
To Lough Neagh, I thought about the rock,
Wanting it. Not for my own salvation;
Hardly at all for me: for sick Belfast,
For the gunmen and the slogan-writers,
For the poor crazy girl I met in the station,
For Kevin and Declan, who would soon mistrust
All camera-carrying strangers. But of course
The thing's already theirs: a monument,
A functionless, archaic, pitted stone
And a few mouthfuls of black rainwater.

FLEUR ADCOCK

Ballymurphy
for Padraic Fiacc

Clothesline sag of the street
With puddles wincing at wind snare.
The foul cribs fidget on concrete;
Eyes claim questions I can't answer
And the ragtime rhythm irks the exegete.
Sky's gravid belly gives birth -
Mist curling on Black Mountain -
Ferns and fieldmice safe from collusion.
Here where the rainbow comes to earth
Heedless children: eyes big as owls
Straddle deformities in shivering pools.

Silence shredded by a seismic scream -
Sleep can't erase the roots of rage.
This low belt of sky brings sudden stars
Like points of light where viewed polemics perish
And daylight trickles to a tender language.

BRENDAN HAMILL

Revolutionary Revolution

Insidious in ways no gunfire touches, revolution
must have revolution in it too,
not be the same old murder.

> The cry for a tender
> style has never been so truly from the heart,
> so treated as nothing much.
>
> GEORGE BUCHANAN

Dissenter at the Harp Festival Belfast 1972

1

A glint of water, and a flash of wing,
A dying history lingers in your touch.
Belfast stirs now, Commerce crowds our streets
Our harbour's thronged with merchant masts,
The future's sure, a New Age dawns -
Reason, Brotherhood, the Rights of Man -
A glint of water and a flash of wing.

2

The sky above those hills seems closer now,
The fields that throw back slanting evening light
Seem brighter, now your music calmly
Moves like water, or a bird in flight,
Seem fresher, earlier and less our own.

3

Blind Harper, blind O'Neill, you conjure us
With sound, you comprehend the wind
The night, sweet waking by a mountain stream
Cold of winter and the patron's fire
High summer and the lover's kiss,
Aristocracy is in your mind, your music
Is a chieftain, bard and clan
Your music is a world that is itself.

4

I'll scour the land for echoes ...

TERENCE BROWN

Bridges and the Blossoms by the River*

After the harsh storms of late spring
The cherry blossom is in bloom again -
In the avenues and by the river bank.

The young spruce trees round the theatre
Spray out a hail storm of fresh green needles.
Below them the river flows silently,
Ignoring the activity round the concrete columns
That rise from the waters, for the new bridge.
Its builders remind me of the builders
Swarming over the girders of the theatre
On a summer such as this five years ago.

Now the stage which was then an earthen plot,
Echoes the words of the poets, the writers,
The weavers of dreams, the tellers of tales;
And vibrates pleasantly from the rhythm of the dance.
From the darkness we walk into the blended lights,
Play our part to a gathering of glowing faces in the shadows,
And to the darkness we return
To be abruptly made aware from time to time
Of the grimmer drama played out in the darkened streets
Of a tortured city -
But through it all the river flows silently.

The intrusion of the conflict, like a sharpened scythe,
Draws close occasionally as the exploding bomb
Shakes a window and wall, and stills an audience in tension,
And tingles the nerves of an actor in his role.
But gradually artist and audience regain communion
With themselves and with each other.

Time's mill wheel turns again,
And the beat of life regains its pace
Smoothly as the blended lighting on the stage,
The dancers dance a sharper vital rhythm in their dance.
Composure is regained again
As the cherry blossom in the street light
Weathers out the torrent, the deluge, and the hail.

So once more the stage survives the discord and the strife,
May the walls of this meeting place, the bridge's span,
And the blossom from the tree, be mirrored long in these deep waters,
For without these what is living, what is striving, what is life?

*Written in April 1973 after an explosion at the Lyric Theatre, Belfast.

JACK McQUOID

The Coasters

You coasted along
to larger houses, gadgets, more machines,
to golf and weekend bungalows,
caravans when the children were small,
the Mediterranean, later, with the wife.

You did not go to church often,
weddings were special;
but you kept your name on the books
against eventualities;
and the parson called, or the curate.

You showed a sense of responsibility,
with subscriptions to worthwhile causes
and service in voluntary organisations,
and, anyhow, this did the business no harm
no harm at all.
Relations were improving. A good
useful life. You coasted along.

You even had a friend or two of the other sort,
coasting too: your ways ran parallel.
Their children and yours seldom met, though,
being at different schools.
You visited each other, decent folk with a sense
of humour. Introduced, even, to
one of their clergy. And then you smiled
in the looking-glass, admiring, a
little moved by, your broadmindedness.
Your father would never have known
one of them. Come to think of it,
when you were young, your own home was never
visited by one of the other sort.

Relations were improving. The annual processions
began to look rather like folk-festivals.

When that noisy preacher started,
he seemed old-fashioned, a survival.
Later you remarked on his vehemence,
a bit on the rough side.
But you said, admit it, you said in the club.
'You know, there's something in what he says.'

And you who seldom had time to read a book,
what with reports and the colour-supplements,
denounced censorship.
And you who never had an adventurous thought
were positive that the church of the other sort
vetoes thought.
And you who simply put up with marriage
for the children's sake, deplored
the attitude of the other sort
to divorce.
You coasted along,
And all the time, though you never noticed,
the old lies festered;
the ignorant became more thoroughly infected;
there were gains, of course;
you never saw any go barefoot.

The government permanent, sustained
by the regular plebiscites of loyalty.
You always voted but never
put a sticker on the car;
a card in the window
would not have been seen from the street.
Faces changed on the posters, names too, often,
but the same families, the same class of people.
A Minister once called you by your first name.
You coasted along
and the sores suppurated and spread.

Now the fever is high and raging;
who would have guessed it, coasting along?
The ignorant-sick thresh about in delirium
and tear at scabs with dirty finger-nails.
The cloud of infection hangs over the city,
a quick change of wind and it
might spill over the leafy suburbs.
You coasted too long.

                       JOHN HEWITT

Rubicon

And once across the river
there is no more retreating,
no matter how many times
    it is recrossed.

Yet a silhouette in the dream
      commands me back,
back into the man storm eye,

the renaissance of steel,
a whirlwind of measures,
the casting of a final spell
      with gun metal.

Valkyrie sweeps the streets,
fire dusting the slums, fired
fuel splashes on flesh,
so I trek into the bushes
because this plague
of mine is everyone's;
it is a black death fever
      in the back streets.

          DENNIS KELLY

Names

They call this 'Black North'
black from the heart out -

it doesn't matter about
particularities when mouths

mumble the handy sayings
and day-in minds tighten.

I've been here having thought
nowhere else was possible,

a condition of destiny, or what
the old generations only fumbled

with: conceit, success, a fair
share of decent hardship,

compounded, forced into fierce
recognition - the card house toppled.

In this extreme, perched
on the edge of the Atlantic

you feel to look down
and gather around the details

thinking to store them away
bundle and pack in the exiles' way -

the faithful journey
of turning your back

like the host of others,
the scholars and saints.

Line up and through the turn-
stile, click the ticket

and wait till you're
clear of it: Glue to

the passport: IRISH POET,
Destination, America or

Early Grave. You need never
recall the other names.

GERALD DAWE

Epilogue

After I helped you tear up
the gangplank from the Law
as I mounted the bus back

into town, and my old umbrella
cracked from an ice-storm wind our
'old acquaintanceship', I

gaped at and prayed to the driver:
'It would be a good idea' he swore
'to let friggin go-of-it!'

Yes, day is night out in
the hail-stone skinning sky
as I watch my broken stick

(all spokes) - fly
down the whimpering street,
your liner far out into

the bitch Atlantic now:
an elongated neck of the snow
-goose in flight ship-horn

honk of the cow in heat,
an art-long, ram-rod flicker
of fingers, then: GONE

Well then, good, great, I love
you all the more because
you are not here ....

                PADRAIC FIACC

Biographies and Index to Poets

FLEUR ADCOCK was born in 1934 in Papakura, New Zealand, and was educated at the Victoria University of Wellington, New Zealand, where she read classics. Her previous collections are *Tigers* (1967), and *High Tide in the Garden* (1971). Her forthcoming collection, *The Scenic Route*, is due shortly from Oxford. It celebrates the centenary of her grandparents' emigration from Ulster in 1874 to New Zealand. She works in London as a librarian in the Foreign and Commonwealth Office.
(See pages 148, 150)

EAVAN BOLAND was born in 1944 in Dublin. She was educated at Trinity College 1962-66; and was on the staff of Trinity from 1967-8. She received the Macaulay Fellowship in Poetry from the Arts Council in 1968. *New Territory* appeared in 1968, and *The War Horse*, a second volume of poems, is coming out with Gollancz next year. She is married to the novelist Kevin Casey, and has been active in bringing opposing forces in Ulster to the conference table.
(See pages 98, 102)

JOHN BOYD was born in East Belfast of working class parents. He was educated at Queen's University, Belfast, and Trinity College, Dublin. He taught English and history in various schools and was Senior Talks Producer at the Northern Ireland BBC from 1947 to 1972. His quartet of plays, *The Assassin* (1969), *The Flats* (1971), *The Farm* (1972) and *Guests* (1974) deal directly with present day Ulster violence.
(See page 7)

MICHAEL BOYLE was born in Belfast in the same neighbourhood as Michael Brophy. They shared the same desk at school. His poetry has been broadcast by the Northern Ireland BBC, and he has published in several Irish periodicals including *Hibernia*. He now lives in the Republic.
(See page 80)

MICHAEL BROPHY was born on the Falls Road in Belfast in 1945. He was educated at St Malachy's College and St Joseph's College of Education (Trench House). He graduated from the Open University in 1973. He is the Head of the Science Department in an Andersonstown school. His poetry has appeared in the *Irish Press (New Irish Writing)*, *Hibernia*, *Aquarius*, *The Honest Ulsterman*, and in the *Belfast Telegraph*. He has also broadcast poetry with the BBC in *New Writing in Ireland* and *Soundings* and with UTV in *Spectrum*. His 'Summer', a study of an Ulster childhood, was broadcast on Northern Ireland BBC in 1974. His published collections are *Words* (with Michael Boyle) and *A Tired Tribe* (Blackstaff Press, 1974).
(See pages 16, 24, 33, 52, 72, 76, 83, 117)

TERENCE BROWN was born in 1944 of Irish parents in China. He was educated at Sullivan Upper School, Holywood, Magee College, Derry, and Trinity College, Dublin, where he is at present lecturer in English Literature. He has published poems in several Irish periodicals and is the author of *Louis MacNeice: Sceptical Vision*. He

TERENCE BROWN (continued)
is at present completing a study of poetry in Ulster entitled *Northern Voices: Poets from Ulster*, to be published by Gill and Macmillan.
(See pages 54, 152)

GEORGE BUCHANAN was born in Kilwaughter, Co Antrim, in 1904. He was educated at Campbell College and Queen's University, Belfast. He was on the editorial staff of the *Times* in the '30s, and was drama critic for the *News Chronicle*, and literary critic for the *Times Literary Supplement*. He served in the RAF during the Second World War. Although known as a novelist he has published several books of poetry: *Conversation with Strangers, Morning Papers*, (Gaberbocchus Press), and *Minute Book of a City* (Carcanet Press, 1972). His work was included in *Ten Irish Poets*, edited by James Simmons (Carcanet Press, 1974).
(See pages 124, 151)

JOE CAMPLISSON was born in Belfast in 1928, the son of a brushmaker. He was educated at St Gall's Public Elementary School. He began work at fourteen as a message boy and then laboured in the pig industry for five years. He had an assortment of labouring jobs until he was 42 years of age. He organised community work in the Turf Lodge area during the 1969 crisis and subsequently trained in community development with Community Relations Commission 1970-1974. He is at present a consultant to Community Development. This is the first time his poetry has been published.
(See page 144)

CIARAN CARSON was born in Belfast in 1948. His first language was Irish. After graduating from Queen's University in 1971 he worked in the Civil Service and is at present teaching in Belfast. He has published a pamphlet, *The Insular Celts* (Ulsterman Publications 1973), and was represented in John Montague's *Faber Book of Irish Verse* (1974). He is at present working on his first book collection.
(See pages 36, 74, 89, 91)

MAURICE JAMES CRAIG was born in Belfast in 1919. He was educated at Magdalene College, Cambridge and at the University of Dublin. He is a much anthologised poet whose poetry has appeared widely in British and Irish periodicals.
(See page 79)

GERALD DAWE born in Belfast in 1952 of working class Protestant people. He was educated at the New University of Ulster, Coleraine. His poetry has appeared in *Atlantis, Lines, Breakthru, New Irish Writing, Lace Curtain, NUU Review, Triangle*, and on BBC Radio 3. He wrote, produced and assisted in their translation into Irish, two prize-winning one-act plays which were performed in Dublin, Galway and Donegal: *The Pawnbroker (An Gaelbrochair)* received an award from *Radio na Gaeltachta*. He worked for a time with the Lyric Youth Theatre in Belfast and as a librarian in the Fine Arts Department of Belfast Central Library. He is at present working on a play about the early stages of William Carleton's life.
(See pages 12, 22, 25, 63, 97, 110, 156)

SEAMUS DEANE was born in Derry in 1940. He studied at Queen's University, Belfast and Cambridge University. After teaching in Derry for two years, he was a Fulbright Lecturer at Reed College in Oregon and a Woodrow Wilson Fellow at the University of California at Berkeley. He is now a lecturer in English at University College, Dublin. His poetry has appeared in many literary magazines and has been widely broadcast. He is the second Ulster poet to be awarded The AE Memorial Prize, granted to him for his first collection, *Gradual Wars* (1972).

SEAMUS DEANE (continued)
(See pages 35, 41, 45, 53, 57, 68, 127)

NORMAN DUGDALE was born in 1921 in Lancashire. He was educated at Manchester University and then entered the Civil Service. He is now Permanent Secretary of Health and Social Services for Northern Ireland, and was awarded an OBE in this year's Birthday Honours. His publications include a Queen's University pamphlet, *The Disposition of the Weather* (1967), *A Prospect of the West* (Barrie & Jenkins, 1970), and *Night Ferry* (Masquer Press, 1974). A larger collection is now with the publishers. He is one of the original members of the Philip Hobsbaum group which first encouraged such Ulster poets as Derek Mahon, Michael Longley, Michael Brophy and Seamus Heaney.
(See pages 8, 13, 14, 143, 146)

PAUL DURCAN was born in Dublin in 1944. His poetry has been widely published in Britain and Ireland. 'Beyond ties of friendship' he writes, 'I have no Ulster connections as such. But like everyone else on this island - in so far as I am a child of this island, I am a child of Ulster too, and everything that happens in Ulster affects me as if affects everyone else here. I can only say that I feel unspeakable admiration for the people of Ulster itself who go on with life and work in spite of all that's happening.' Paul Durcan, who is now living in Cork, received the Patrick Kavanagh Award in 1974.
(See page 131)

DESMOND EGAN was born in Athlone and educated at Mullingar and at University College, Dublin, where he obtained an MA in 1965. His first collection, *Midland*, was published in 1973 and his second collection, *Poems 1974*, is due shortly. He is the co-author, with Eoghan O Tuairisc (Eugene Watters) of a book of poetry criticism, *Focus* (Fallons, 1972). He has edited *Poiemata*, an anthology of poetry (1972), and, with Michael Hartnett, *Choice*, an anthology of contemporary Irish poetry (1973). He founded the Goldsmith Press in 1972. He edited a special edition of *The Deserted Village* for the Goldsmith Bi-centenary Year (1974).
(See page 105)

CONLETH ELLIS was born in Carlow in 1937. He was educated at the University Colleges at Dublin and Galway. He taught in Belfast from 1960-1968, and now lives in Athlone. His publications are, *This Ripening Time* (1966) and *Under the Stone* (1972). His first collection in Irish is due to be published shortly.
(See pages 68, 81, 83)

PADRAIC FIACC was born in the Lower Falls Road, Belfast, in 1924. He spent his childhood on East Street in the 'Markets' area. His father was forced to emigrate to the United States, and he was educated in New York City at Commerce and Haaren High Schools, Manhattan, and St Joseph's Seminary, Calicoon, New York State. He returned to Belfast in 1946. He was the first Ulster poet to receive the AE Prize (for an unpublished collection, *Woe to the Boy* (1957)). *By the Black Stream* was published by the Dolmen Press in 1969 and *Odour of Blood* by the Goldsmith Press in 1973. A forthcoming collection is at present with the publishers.
(See pages 17, 21, 28, 37, 69, 77, 79, 82, 84, 86, 87, 90, 94, 95, 98, 101, 103, 109, 111, 118, 157)

MICHAEL FOLEY was born in Derry in 1947. He was educated at St Columb's College and at Queen's University, Belfast. He has published two pamphlets, *Heil Hitler* (1969) and *The Acne and the Ecstasy* (1973) (Ulsterman Publications). He is at present teaching at a Catholic school in London, and he is a regular contribu-

MICHAEL FOLEY (continued)
tor to *Fortnight*. His work appeared in James Simmons' *Ten Irish Poets* (Carcanet Press 1974). He has written a play about the Burntollet march.
(See page 109)

MICHAEL FRIEL, the Derry poet, is 26. He is the son of the composer, Redmond Friel. His poetry has been published in *Threshold, Hibernia,* and *The Honest Ulsterman,* and he has written book reviews for various Irish periodicals. He is at present living in Italy.
(See page 49)

PATRICK GALVIN was born in Cork in 1929 and emigrated at an early age. He served in the RAF in North Africa during the war. He was a winner of the Lyric Theatre's Leverhulme Drama Fellowship. His *Nightfall to Belfast* was produced at the Lyric in 1973 and his *The Last Burning* in 1974. He is at present poetry editor of *Threshold*. He has published three collections: *Heart of Grace, Christ in London* and *The Wood Burners* (New Writers' Press, 1973). He has also appeared in *Five Irish Poets* (Mercier Press, 1970).
(See page 134)

ROBERT GREACEN was born in Derry in 1920. He was educated at Queen's University and at Trinity College, Dublin. He co-edited, with Valentin Iremonger, the *Faber Book of Irish Verse*, and was a contributor to *The Bell* and *Horizon*. He was one of the leaders of the school of Ulster poets of the '40s. His published works are *One Recent Evening* (1944), *The Undying Day* (1948), and an autobiographical book, *Even Without Irene* (1969). He writes reviews for *Books and Bookmen*, the *Listener* and *Hibernia*, and a new collection of his 'Captain Fox' poems is due from the Gallery Press shortly.
(See pages 19, 20, 43, 144)

BRENDAN HAMILL was born in 1945 in Belfast. He was educated at St Thomas', Ballymurphy and the New University of Ulster, Coleraine. He did community work during the internment crisis in Ballymurphy in 1971. His work has been published in the *Irish Times, Phoenix,* the *Belfast Telegraph,* the *Irish Independent, Tamarisk* and the New Ulster University review, *Triangle,* and has been broadcast by BBC Northern Ireland and RTE. He is at present working on a first collection.
(See pages 118, 121, 151)

SEAMUS HEANEY was born in Co Derry in 1939. He was educated at St Columb's College, Derry and Queen's University, Belfast. His publications are *Death of a Naturalist* (1966), *Door into the Dark* (1969) and *Wintering Out* (1972), and he edits *Soundings* for Blackstaff Press. He is the most popular and widely known of the Ulster poets, and the prizes he has won include the Eric Gregory Trust Award (1966), the Cholmondeley Award (1967), the Somerset Maugham Award (1968), the Denis Devlin Award (1972) and the American Irish Foundation Award (1972). He is at present working on a new collection, which includes several of the poems in this anthology.
(See pages 3, 38, 42, 44, 45, 46, 51, 65, 67)

JOHN HEWITT was born in Belfast in 1907, and was educated at Queen's University. He was on the staff of the Belfast Museum and Art Gallery from 1930 to 1957, and was Art Director of the Herbert Art Gallery and Museum, Coventry, until his recent retirement and return to Belfast. He first emerged as a major figure during the flowering of Ulster poetry in the '40s. His work has appeared widely in many anthologies and he has published several volumes of poetry. His *Collected Poems* appeared in

JOHN HEWITT (continued)
1968, followed by *An Ulster Reckoning* in 1972. His new collection, *Out of My Time*, was published by Blackstaff Press in 1974.
(See pages 1, 4, 6, 8, 9, 11, 13, 17, 51, 76, 81, 145, 154)

JACK HOLLAND was born in Belfast in 1947. He was educated at the University of Essex and at Trinity College, Dublin. His work has been published in *Ariel, The Honest Ulsterman* and the *Irish Press (New Irish Writing)*.
(See page 147)

DENNIS KELLY was born in Belfast in 1952, and educated at Queen's University. He has been published in the *Irish Press (New Irish Writing)*, *Hibernia, Harangue, Fortnight* and various university magazines. He lives in north Belfast and has also lived in London, France and Italy. He is preparing a forthcoming first collection.
(See pages 59, 99, 114, 155)

JOHNSTON KIRKPATRICK was born in Belfast and worked as a tradesman in the shipyard and building industry. After living in England for ten years he has returned to Northern Ireland and has recently graduated at the New University of Ulster, Coleraine. His work has been published in several periodicals. He is considered one of the most promising of the emerging new Ulster poets.
(See page 31)

JAMES LIDDY was born in County Clare in 1934. He practised for some years as a barrister in Dublin before abandoning this for poetry. He founded and edited the literary magazine *Arena*, and has published several collections, *Esau, My Kingdom for a Drink, A Blue Smoke*, and *Blue Mountain* (Dolmen Press). His latest collection, *A Munster Song of Love and War*, was published by the White Rabbit Press, San Francisco, in 1971. He is at the moment translating Baudelaire and teaching at Galway University. He taught for several years in the United States.
(See page 138)

GERRY LOCKE is a teenager who lives and works in north Belfast. He was educated at Stella Maris High School. This is the first time his poetry has appeared in print.
(See page 52)

MICHAEL LONGLEY was born in Belfast in 1939. He was educated at Trinity College in Dublin. He was co-winner with Derek Mahon of the Gregory Award. His published collections are *No Continuing City* (1969) and *An Exploded View* (1973). He was formerly poetry critic of the *Irish Times*, and his work has appeared in the *Listener*, the *New Statesman*, and many other British and Irish periodicals and has been broadcast by the BBC. He has edited an anthology of Ulster children's poetry. He works for the Arts Council of Northern Ireland, and is married to the critic, Edna Longley.
(See pages 12, 21, 96, 104, 129)

LIAM LYNCH was born in 1949 in Co Down. He was educated by the Passionist Fathers and at Stranmillis College, Belfast. He is at present employed by the Northern Ireland Civil Service. He has had work published by the *Irish Press (New Irish Writing)* and *The Honest Ulsterman*. He is at present preparing a first collection.
(See page 147)

ROY McFADDEN was born in Belfast in 1921 during the 'troubles', where he lived until the blitz in 1941 'when a bomb sent him to Downpatrick'. He was associated with Robert Greacen and John Hewitt in the Ulster poetry flowering of the '40s.

ROY McFADDEN (continued)
His collections are *Swords and Ploughshares* (1943), *Flowers for a Lady* (1945), *The Heart's Townland* (1947), *Elegy for the Dead of the Princess Victoria* (1953), and *The Garryowen* (1972). He edited the Ulster literary magazine, *Rann*. A forthcoming collection is to be published shortly. He works as a Belfast solicitor.
(See pages 18, 84, 119, 142, 149)

JAMES McFARLAND was born in Belfast in 1950 of a Greek mother and an Ulster father. He was educated at Cardiff University. He has worked in the Northern Ireland Civil Service, and is now training as a teacher at Stranmillis College, Belfast. He lives in Lisburn with his wife, Dorothy.
(See page 64)

GERALD McFLYNN was born in 1947 in Magherafelt, Co Derry. He was educated at St Patrick's High School, Downpatrick, Queen's University and St Patrick's College, Maynooth. He was ordained as a priest in 1973. He has had poems published in the *Irish Independent* and *The Tablet*.
(See page 36)

MICHAEL McGINLEY was born in Derry in 1943. His poems, 'Parting' and 'Living 1974' were first published in David Marcus's *New Irish Writing* (the *Irish Press*) in August 1974.
(See page 138)

TOM McGURK was born in 1946 in Dublin. He was educated at Catholic and Protestant schools and later at Queen's University. He was a founder member of the People's Democracy. He lived in Northern Ireland during the first upsurge of violence and was one of the original Burntollet marchers. He now works in Dublin as a freelance writer, broadcaster and journalist. In 1972, he won a Jacob's Radio Award for his evocative documentary on Belfast entitled *Between the Mountain and the Gantries* and his television documentary about the North, *Down There*, has been shown in eight countries. Both were *Prix Italia* entries in the Venice Festival.
(See pages 34, 66)

JAMES McKENNA is a working-class poet, sculptor, and playwright residing in Dublin. His play *Ulster Lies Bleeding* was first produced in the old Project Gallery, in 1972. RTE broadcast his play *Hotep comes from River* in 1969, but he is best known for his *The Scatterin'*, a success in the Dublin Theatre Festival of 1960 which played in London in 1962. His masque play *At Bantry* was performed in the Peacock Theatre in 1967 and was published by Scepter Books in 1968. His first collection of poetry, *Poems*, was published by Goldsmith Press last year.
(See page 107)

TOM McLAUGHLIN teaches in Belfast. His collection, *So Far No Surprises*, was brought out by Ulsterman Publications in 1971. His work was included in the anthology *Choice*, published by Goldsmith Press in 1973. His work has been published in Irish literary magazines, but he is chiefly known as one of *The Honest Ulsterman* poets.
(See page 127)

TREVOR McMAHON was educated at Queen's University. He co-edits the poetry magazine, *Caret*, with William Peskett.
(See page 2)

MAOL MACMULLEN is a painter and poet. He lives in Co Down.
(See pages 115, 140)

JACK McQUOID was born in Liverpool in 1910. His mother came from Co Tyrone and his father from Co Antrim. He moved to Belfast after the First World War, and attended the Technical College and worked in the shipyard. During the depression of 1930 he emigrated to California, but returned to Ireland in 1933 to take up acting and broadcasting. He contributed verse to *Ireland Today* and the *New English Weekly*. He served in the RAF during the Second World War, and later took up farming in Co Down. He contributed poetry to *The Bell, Lagan, Rann* and *Poetry Ireland*. His first collection, *Followers of the Plough*, appeared in 1949. He is at present acting with the Lyric Players and has contributed poetry to the magazine, *Threshold*.
(See page 152)

ARTHUR McVEIGH is a teenager. His 'Thought on the Derry Riots' first appeared in Michael Longley's anthology of young people's writing in Ulster, *Under the Moon and Over the Stars* (Arts Council of Northern Ireland, 1971).
(See page 47)

GEORGE McWHIRTER was born in Belfast and educated at Queen's University. He teaches at the University of British Columbia, Vancouver. His first collection, *Catalan Poems*, was brought out in 1971 by Canadian Young Poets.
(See page 9)

DEREK MAHON was born in Belfast in 1941, and educated at Trinity College, Dublin. His collections are *Night Crossing* (1968), *Beyond Howth Head* (1970), and *Lives* (1972). He now lives in London where he is on the staff of *Vogue*. He edited *The Sphere Book of Modern Irish Poetry* (1972).
(See pages 15, 23, 93, 123, 132)

TOM MATTHEWS was born in Ballymena in 1945 and brought up in Derry. He 'survived his schooling by keeping very quiet'. He lives quietly in Larne and works quietly in industry. His poems have appeared in *New Irish Writing* (the *Irish Press*) and *The Honest Ulsterman*. He has published two pamphlets, *Interior Din* (1969) and *Foolstop* (1973), both Ulsterman Publications. His first collection, *Doctor Wilson as an Arab*, is to be published shortly. His work has also appeared in James Simmons' *Ten Irish Poets* (1974, Carcanet Press).
(See page 126)

HUGH MAXTON was born in 1947 in Wicklow and educated at Trinity College, Dublin. He spent some time in Germany in 1968, and then moved to Derry at the start of the troubles. He founded the review *Atlantis* with Seamus Deane and Derek Mahon in 1970. He lectured in Anglo-Irish literature at Magee College, Derry and at the New University of Ulster, and is now teaching in Leeds. His poems have appeared in *Ariel, Aquarius, Atlantis, The Honest Ulsterman,* the *Malahat Review* and the *Transatlantic Review*. His first collection, *Stones*, appeared in 1970, published by Allen Figgis.
(See pages 60, 135)

TERENCE MAXWELL was born in Jersey City, USA, in 1951. He was educated at Bard College and studied Irish at the New University of Ulster, Coleraine. He is at present living in Belfast and teaching in County Derry. His poems and translations

TERENCE MAXWELL (continued)
have appeared in a number of periodicals in America, including *Corfu, The Muse, Symposium* and *Ycelpt*.
(See pages 55, 70, 75, 88)

PATRICK MAYBIN was born in Lisburn in 1916. He studied medicine at Queen's University, Belfast (where he edited *The New Northman*.) He served with distinction in the Royal Army Medical Corps in North Africa and Italy during World War II. His poetry and prose reportage have appeared in many Irish periodicals and journals and he is represented in many anthologies. He is at present Medical Advisor to the Central Services.
(See page 10)

EWART MILNE was born in 1903 in Dublin. He worked at a number of jobs: sailor, teacher, works clerk, journalist, and estate manager. He was in Spain during the Civil War, where he worked as a Medical Aid volunteer on the government side. He is the most outspoken of the Irish poets on Ulster affairs, identifying himself with the rights of the Protestant minority in the Republic and the aspirations and loyalties of the Protestant majority in the North. He has published over ten collections of poetry and is represented in the *Oxford Book of Irish Verse* and the more recent *Faber Book of Irish Verse*.
(See page 10)

JOHN MONTAGUE was born in Brooklyn in 1929. He was educated at the National University, Dublin, but his childhood and early youth were spent in Co Tyrone. His collections are *Poisoned Lands* (1961), *A Chosen Light* (1967), *Tides* (1970), and *The Rough Field* (1972). He edited the *Faber Book of Irish Verse* (1974). He lived for some years in Paris and has lectured in the United States. He teaches at the University of Cork.
(See pages 5, 7, 85, 102)

PAUL MULDOON was born in Co Armagh in 1951. He was educated at Queen's University, Belfast. His collections are *Knowing My Place* (1971, Ulsterman Publications), *Poetry Introduction 2* (1972, Faber), and *New Weather* (1973, Faber). His work has also appeared in the *Newman Review, The Tablet*, and the *Listener*. He works for the Northern Ireland BBC in Belfast. He is considered one of the most promising and distinguished of the younger Ulster poets.
(See pages 139, 141)

ELEANOR MURRAY was born in Banbridge, Co Down. She was educated at Banbridge Academy where she started writing poetry, and then at St Mary's College of Education, Belfast. She taught for some years, and three and a half years ago resumed writing poetry as an escape from the political situation. Her poems have appeared in the *Irish Times*, the *Irish Press* and *Threshold*, and groups of them have been broadcast on two occasions from Radio Eireann. She is at present finishing a first collection of poems.
(See pages 41, 64)

PAUL MURRAY is a Belfastman who was ordained to the priesthood in 1973. He was educated at Tallaght. He is at present doing advanced studies in theology in Rome. His collection, *Ritual Poems*, came out in 1971.
(See page 105)

JOAN NEWMANN lives in Co Down. She published *First Letter Home* (Belfast, Festival Publication, 1966). Her poetry has been broadcast by the Northern Ireland

JOAN NEWMANN (continued)
BBC and has also appeared in several Irish literary magazines.
(See page 108)

FRANK ORMSBY was born in Co Fermanagh in 1947. He was educated at Queen's University. He is the editor of *The Honest Ulsterman*. He has published two pamphlets, *Ripe for Company* (1971) and *Business as Usual* (1973). He teaches in a Belfast grammar school. He received the Gregory Award in 1974.
(See pages 115, 137)

STEWART PARKER lives in Belfast and commutes to Cornell University every year, where he lectures. He is well known for several other literary activities as well as being a poet: including his broadcasts on the Northern Ireland BBC as a book critic, his reviews of Pop for the *Irish Times*, and for editing the late Sam Thompson's *Over the Bridge* for Gill & Macmillan. His long awaited canto sequence is to be published this year and he has published two pamphlets via Festival Publications: *The Casualty's Meditation* (1966) and *Maw* (1968). His interesting use of free verse and surrealistic word patterns has somewhat unfairly ostracised him from the more conventional Ulster poets' circle.
(See page 125)

WILLIAM PESKETT was educated at Cambridge. He is the co-editor of *Caret*. A selection of his poetry has been published by Faber in their *Introduction 2*. His poetry has appeared in several Irish literary magazines and he is considered one of the most promising of the younger Ulster poets.
(See page 127)

WILLIAM J PHILBIN born Kiltimagh in 1907. He was educated at Ballaghaderreen and Maynooth, where he became Professor of Dogmatic Theology. He was formerly Bishop of Clonfert, and is now Bishop of Down and Connor (Belfast). Apart from his writings on theological and social subjects, he has published *Mise Padraig*, a translation into Irish of the writings of St Patrick, and an edition in Irish of *Aeneid II*. His translations from the Greek, *To You Simonides*, were brought out last year by Dolmen Press, Dublin. He was a contributor to *Latin Poetry in Verse Translation*, edited by L R Lind (Houghton Mifflin, Boston) and *The Greek Anthology*, edited by Peter Jay (Allen Lane, Penguin). He has had translations and original poems published in *The Tablet*, the *Belfast Telegraph*, the *Spectator*, and the *Observer*.
(See page 99)

PP is the pen-name of a Lisburn teenager who is at present studying at Queen's University, Belfast. This is his first published poem.
(See page 115)

META MAYNE REID is a broadcaster and writer Her poetry has appeared in *The Field, Country Life, Hibernia,* the *Glasgow Herald,* the *Irish Press,* the *Irish Times,* and many earlier, if short-lived Ulster periodicals such as *Rann*, the late Denis Ireland's *The Ulsterman*, G B Newe's *Glensman* and some Youth Hostel magazines. (She is a founder-member of the Northern Ireland Youth Hostels Association and is now president of the Northern Ireland PEN.) She won the Listowel Writers' Poetry Prize and Trophy Award in 1974. *No Ivory Tower* was recited by a Latvian friend at the Taipei Poets' Congress in China recently and translated into Latvian with several of her other poems. Twenty two of her children's books have been published by Macmillan and Faber. She lives in Crawfordsburn near Bangor. Her poetry collection, *No Ivory Tower*, was brought out by Outposts Press this year.

META MAYNE REID (continued)
(See pages 1, 95, 103, 104, 114, 124)

JAMES SIMMONS was born in Derry in 1933 and was educated at Leeds University. His collections are *Late But In Earnest* (1967), *In the Wilderness* (1969), *Energy to Burn* (1971), *No Land is Waste, Dr Eliot* (1972), and *The Long Summer Still to Come* (1973). He edited the anthology *Ten Irish Poets* (1974), and a forthcoming collection, *West Strand Visions*, is due from the Blackstaff Press. He taught at the Friends' School in Lisburn for several years and in Nigeria. He founded *The Honest Ulsterman* in 1968, which first published many of the younger and less known Ulster poets. He is a song-writer and singer in his own right. He also lectures in drama and Anglo-Irish literature at the New University of Ulster, Coleraine. He has given poetry readings of his own work in Canada and Germany.
(See pages 72, 74, 92, 110, 134)

OLIVER SNODDY (Padraig O Snodaigh) was born in Carlow in 1935 of Ulster Protestant stock on his father's side. He is President of the Chonradh na Gaeilge. He won the Butler Foundation Prize with his book, *Comhghuaillithe na Reabhloide, 1913-1916*. He has published three collections of poetry in collaboration with other poets. He is editor of *Pobal*. He has recently published a booklet, *Hidden Ulster*, on the Irish cultural background of the Ulster Protestant. His work has appeared in many academic periodicals, including *Studia Hibernica, The Irish Sword, Capuchin Annual, North Munster Antiquarian Journal*, and *An Cosantoir*.
(See page 27)

GEOFFREY SQUIRES was born in 1942. He was brought up in Donegal. He taught for some time at the University of Isfahan in Persia. His poetry has appeared in several Irish periodicals including *The Honest Ulsterman*. He has a collection at the moment with the publishers.
(See page 137)

W B STANFORD was born in Belfast in 1916. He was educated at Trinity College, Dublin. He was editor of *Hermathena* from 1942-1962. He is a poet and Greek scholar, and his contribution to the understanding of ancient Greek literature has been outstanding. He is the author of many books on Greek literature. He is at present living in Dublin.
(See page 123)

PATRIC STEVENSON was born in Sussex in 1909 of Irish parents. He has lived in the North of Ireland since 1920. He was educated at Methodist College, Belfast, at the Belfast College of Arts, and at the Slade School, London. He is a landscape painter, and has been President of the Royal Ulster Academy since 1970. He published his first book of poems, *Flowing Water* (Falcon Press, London) in 1945. He has published poems in *Irish Voices, The Bell*, the *Irish Times*, the *Belfast Telegraph, Outposts, Phoenix, New English Weekly, Country Life, Caret*, and *Pegasus*. He is currently writing a book on music dealing with some of the important 78 rpm gramophone records issued between the wars.
(See page 48)

W T STEVENSON is a Belfast Leading Fireman. His poems have been broadcast on the Northern Ireland BBC and published in *City Week* and *The Parnassian*, the official organ of the Calder Valley Poets' Society. He is also the author of several radio plays.
(See page 106)

FRANCIS STUART was born in Australia in 1902 of Ulster stock. He married Maud Gonne's daughter, Iseult, in 1920. He fought in the Irish Civil War of the 1920s on the Republican side. He lectured on Irish and English literature at Berlin University during the Second World War. Although a fine poet, he is more widely known for his many novels, several of which are now being re-issued by Martin Brian & O'Keefe of London, namely *Redemption, The Pillar of Cloud* and the well-known *Blacklist Section H*. His *Memorial* became a best-seller in the Republic recently.
(See page 46)

VICTOR THOMPSON was born in Derry in 1951. He was educated at Foyle College and Lurgan College. He plays the guitar and writes songs and has appeared with James Simmons at the Lyric Theatre, Queen's Festival and on the BBC. Both poets have established a weekly poetry/music evening in a pub in Portrush.
(See page 77)

SHAUN TRAYNOR was born near Garvagh in Co Derry in 1941. He was educated at Queen's University and at Gypsy Hill College in Surrey. He has written many children's stories for television and has worked as a teacher. He has published short stories in the *Irish Press* and his collection, *The Hardening Ground*, was published in 1974 by Martin, Brian & O'Keefe.
(See pages 29, 97)

ANDREW WATERMAN was born in London in 1940. He worked in clerical and manual jobs for six years, and was educated at Leicester and Oxford universities. He has been lecturing in the Department of English at the New University of Ulster, Coleraine, since 1968 and during that period has been writing and publishing poetry which has appeared in *Stand*, the *Listener, Encounter*, the *Irish Press, Transatlantic Review*, and many other periodicals, in PEN and other anthologies, and has been broadcast. His first collection, *Living Room*, was published by the Marvell Press in 1974 and was the Poetry Book Society's Christmas choice.
(See pages 61, 107, 122)

ANDREW WHITTAKER is a 33 year old Ulster-born poet. He works on the staff of the *Irish Times*. He has had poetry published in *Icarus*, the *Irish Times*, and the *Kilkenny Magazine*.
(See page 133)

PATRICK WILLIAMS was born in Newcastle, Co Down in 1949 and educated 'by devouring any book I could get my hands on. Apart from writing poems, I'm happily unemployed.' He is one of the younger and most original of the new Ulster poets.
(See pages 15, 58, 91, 140)

PAUL YATES is a painter as well as a poet. His first collection, *A White Cat With a Human Face*, appeared in 1974 in a limited edition with drawings by the poet.
(See page 137)

Index to Titles and First Lines

A Belfastman Abroad Argues with Himself: 13
A boar snouted: 52
A Constable Calls: 46
A Fable: 127
A glint of water, and a flash of wing: 152
A Lack of Beauty in our Lives: 107
A long narrow room with four blue: 7
'A real horse of a man,' McTaggart: 34
A rust red jelly: 76
A Slight 'Hitch': 77
A Soldier's Son: 98
A staff nurse through the sleeping ward: 143
A stranger from the past reveals: 137
A town tolling bell, a fatal joke: 59
A young man's war it is, a young man's war: 98
Across the Water: 115
Across the water plains: 114
Admit the fact, you might have stood your ground: 13
After Derry 30 January 1972: 57
After I helped you tear up: 157
After the bombing the British soldier: 101
After the harsh storms of late spring: 152
Against Oncoming Civil War: 17
Alone now: 91
An Ulster Garland: 122
An Ulster Prophecy: 7
An Ulsterman (1969): 81
An Ulsterman in England Remembers: 9
An Urgent Letter: 135
And did we come into our own: 21
And now: 66
And once across the river: 155
Another View of a Pig: 52
Apology: 59
Arraigned by silence, I recall: 35
As a Child in Derry: 43
As a child in Derry I heard the shots: 43
As I denied his name: 91
As I was walking round the streets of Derry: 47

As It Should Be: 93
At high tide the sea is under the city: 115
At Port-na-happle: 63
At 69 Alliance Road, Belfast: 1967: 31
Autumn 1939: 19

Ballad to a Traditional Refrain: 79
Ballykinlar: May 1940: 10
Ballymurphy: 151
Bear in mind these dead: 145
Before: 77
Before Salamis: 123
Belfast makes a tall boy: 79
Belfast Street 1974: 114
Belfast Teenager 1974: 115
Between the year of the slump and the sell-out, I: 82
Big Ned: 34
Bitter Harvest: 41
Black Cat: 12
Black Hole: 94
Bogside, Derry, 1971: 51
Bonfire: 41
Born in this island, maimed by history: 8
Breaking: 2
Bridges and the Blossoms by the River: 152
British, more or less; Anglican, of a kind: 148
Burnt Offerings: 66
Business it Seems is Still Business: 127
But here the idiom's Lowland Scots: 8

Cage under Siege: 15
Cave: 85
Child of our Time: 102
Childrens' Games: 97
Christ Goodbye: 90
Civil War: 45
Claudy: 74
Clinical Notes (extract): 143
Close by my kitchen window juts: 122
Clothesline sag of the street: 151
Coup de Grace 1973: 21

Daisymount Terrace: 18

Dance Little Man: 83
Dandering home from work at mid: 90
Dark Night of the Mill Hag: 87
Death in the Glen: 16
Derry: 53
Derry Images, 1968-71: 61
Derry, Londoned Derry, jerry-built: 61
Derry Student Before and After: 77
Dissenter at the Harp Festival Belfast 1972: 152
Docker: 67
Downpatrick: 142
Downpatrick Mental Hospital: 140
'Drink water from the hollow in the stone ...': 150
Dull Spring Cantata: 114
Dumping (left over from the autumn): 98
Dying Truth: 106

Edvard Munch: 123
Elegy in 'The Holy Land': 28
Emigrant Brother: 121
Emigrants, Refugees: 118
Empty Raft: 110
Enemies: 79
Enemy Encounter: 98
English Class: 83
Epilogue: 157
Even the barflies move to corner tables: 137
Experience: 110
Eyes running together: 94

Falls Funeral: 102
Fear: 64
Fitts: 125
Floods: 115
For Giles Gordon: 104
For my mother I would build a monument: 29
For Sean Cassidy, d. 24.2.1972: 68
For Tom and Ann, Leaving: 117
From Carrigskeewaun in Killadoon: 129
From the school in the Church Quarter: 18
From the photographs of bleach-greens: 89

Getting Home: 140
Ghosts: 95
Girl with the whooping cough: 28
Glass Grass: 111
Glengormley: 15
Glowing with the school-empty screech: 86

God is too much the way he asks of me: 41
God no, please!: 115
Guns for the Boys: 72

He is not purged: 70
Heil Hitler: 109
Here are two pictures from my father's head-: 96
Here at a distance, rocked by hopes and fears: 9
Here, often, a man provoked has said his say: 17
Here's a song for Gerry Kelly: 92
Heritages: 25
His bicycle stood at the windowsill, its fat black: 46
How strange we are sitting here: 138
Hymn 1969: 48

I am haunted by ghosts: 95
I am of Northern Ireland: born: 84
I'm writing just after an encounter: 38
I do not envy those: 124
I hear the street names on the radio: 11
I know the cobwebbed squint: 9
I ranged Donegall Street, she said: 99
I remember the dour walls: 22
I saw the Pope breaking stones on Friday: 7
I Used to Live: 63
I used to smile: 64
'I want to fight you,' he said in a Belfast accent: 110
I was subjugated under arches, manumitted at a: 44
I Won't Dance: 84
Icon: 118
In Belfast, Europe, your man: 84
In better days the road: 80
In fortunate places: 119
In Kilroot, Co Antrim in search of Swift: 147
In the brow sweat of racked flesh: 31
In the ward's white and blue: 140
In the wood of self-killers: 60
In this dream I am carrying a pig: 12
In this Year of Grace: 76
Insidious in ways no gunfire touches, revolution: 151
Internee: 37
Irish Dead: 58
Irish kids sneer and jeer: 95
Is it just like picking a lock: 74
It is not absolutely fair: 37

171

It is the season of death: 107
It's not 'These People': 144
It seemed such a cheap: 103
It was an ease for her to die they said: 27

July: 45

Keeping My Place: 119
Kids at War: 95
Kids down on hunkers: 97
Kindertotenlieder: 104
Known for your sausages: 16

Lars: 146
Leaning forward I watch how the: 1
Letter to Derek Mahon: 21
Letter to Seamus Heaney: 129
Lightnings slaughtered: 57
Like the hero in an old-time novel: 64
Linen: 89
Live Games: 97
Looking out across the playground: 97

March: 149
McFadden hawked 'Peace News' in Royal Avenue: 19
Meditations on the Suspension of Stormont 1972: 29
Miles of high-wire fencing: 36
Modes of expression pass: 133
My grandfather was a blacksmith: 33

Names: 156
Nan: 27
Neither an Elegy nor a Manifesto: 145
New Year's Eve 1969: 13
Night-Ferry: 14
Nightmare: 12
No Ivory Tower: 124
No Truck (extract): 49
Northern Ireland Late Night News: 76
Not a neighbourhood of fashion: 75
Note on Passing (extract): 70
Nothing but the Truth: 64
Nothing was more under a cloud than a tempting prospect: 124
Now that two storey Tiger's Bay: 88

Old Men's Letters: 88
On the Grand Canal, Thinking of the 'Two Nations': 1
Once again, with creased forehead: 5
Once Alien Here (1942): 6

Once alien here my fathers built their house: 6
Once, under a haystack, young rats: 108
One Day in August: 144
One day in August, going by bus to Annalong: 144
One standing on the empty beach: 10
Orion marching westward still: 10
Outside Looking In: 36

Paleface mirrored in the window grime: 125
Parting: 138
perhaps the first stone: 49
Peter: 91
Pink of a broken cherry-spray: 105
Please Identify Yourself: 148
Poem in Belfast: 23
Poets, is not this solitary man's own: 131
Poets Today: 134
Prolegomena (extract): 8
Protest Poems: 52
Provincial Down: 147

Rage for Order: 132
Rat's Lot: 108
Raid: 68
Reading Keats in Derry City: 46
Reared in the iron rods: 24
Red brick in the suburbs, white horse on the wall: 79
Report of the Tribunal (extract): 55
Revolutionary Revolution: 151
Ring out the old, ring in the new: 13
Riot: 105
Rites: 105
Romanist: 44
Rubicon: 155

Salmon silvering grey to die: 17
Search: 54
September deepens and the nights are long: 46
She scarcely speaks: 103
She shrieks like a bird hiccuping: 87
Sheepman: 137
Shielded, vague soldiers, visored, crouch alert: 51
Silk of the Kine?: 1
Singing School (extract): 42
Sit down, O men of God!: 48
Sitting at my desk among papers: 134
Smallchurch an aquarium of air: 118
So this is, Jimmy, where we live: 135

Soldiers in the hills now: 54
Some day I will go to Aarhus: 3
Somewhere beyond: 132
Son of a Gun: 82
Song for Sinn Fein for Serena: 138
Spotweld: 75

Stele for a Northern Republican: 5
Stoned cheek turned again: 149
Street Names: 11
Summer 1970: 107

Taking, giving back their lives: 141
Tears: 101
Testament: 22
That Stranger: 137
The Ballad of Gerry Kelly, Newsagent: 92
The Ballad of Ranger Best: 72
The beach: 138
The big man with the gun: 72
The Bomb Disposal: 74
The Brethren: 35
The British Connection: 84
The Bullaun: 150
The Coasters: 154
The Dilemma (1969): 8
The drumming started in the cool of the evening: 45
The Field Hospital: 141
The Forge: 33
The glass glitters in the gutter: 114
The Glorious Twelfth: 20
The grounds are very neatly kept: 140
The Hero: 69
The houses in Irish Street: 142
The howl of the rain beating on the military tin: 109
The Indians on Alcatraz: 139
The Iron Circle: 17
The Kickers: 86
The land is banked: 41
The Maze: 36
The Military are tearing down: 21
The Night Air: 137
The night-air knows us, follows: 137
The night-sky red, crackle and roar of flame: 76
The Nightowl: 127
The nightowl preys: 127
The Other Side: 65
The path of reason's very safe: 109
The peacock stands above the farmyard muck: 68
The people: 2

The Persian galleys plumed with warriors: 123
The Reina Del Mar: 9
The rifled honeycomb: 85
The Right to Work: 117
The Scar: 4
The scorched cloth smell and smell of burnt flesh: 112
The shadows-produce of a low, full sun: 147
The Singing Lady: 126
The Snatch: 103
The Sperrins surround it, the Faughan flows by: 74
The sun may shine even on a child's coffin: 104
The Tollund Man: 3
The unemployment in our bones: 53
The way I feel it coming: 45
The Whin Bush: 1
The Women's Tale (extract): 99
The Wrong Ones: 99
There can be no songs for dead children: 104
There, in the corner, staring at his drink: 67
There she stood: 106
There's not a chance now that I might recover: 4
'These People': 144
They call this 'Black North': 156
They said 'Dance little man,': 83
They said you would be back soon: 121
Thigh-deep in sedge and marigolds: 65
This is home. This is the Irish North: 15
This is my country. If my people came: 81
this is my fear: 105
This morning the buses were halted: 55
Thoughts on the Derry Riots: 47
Three Year Old: Belfast 1972: 103
Through time their sharp features: 139
To take an unmeasured leap: 127
To this land of postponed death: 99
Trial Runs: 51
Tribute to a Reporter in Belfast: 131
Troubled City: 80
Two Psalms from Derry: 60

Ulster Ritual: 91
Ulster 71: 99
Ulster Today: 134
Under a Cloud: 124
Under a grey sky, in the ruined church: 147

Under a lunar menses - kite and flame: 58
Under Orion: 10
Unholy Mother Ireland banging: 118
Unmarked faces: 102

Visit to a School: 7

Walking among my own this windy morning: 23
Ways of Failing: 133
We glint like metal fish: 36
We hunted the mad bastard: 93
We saw her in Linenhall Street: 126
We wanted to think it was the quarry: 77
Welcome home ye lads of the Eighth Army: 51
Well, as Kavanagh said, we have lived: 42
Weep far away, quietly: 83
What need have you to ring the bell: 146
What they say about the lyric poet: 127

Whatever you say, say nothing: 38
When it gets darker: 12
When you have everything: 68
Where Are My People Now?: 24
White with argument from the forenoon: 69
Why must the gun be used?: 52
Winking headlands dowsed by dawn: 14
Wonders are many and none is more wonderful than man: 15
Would have taken: 25
Wounds: 96

Yesterday I knew no lullaby: 102
You coasted along: 154
You men of Ulster, can you spare the time: 72
You tramped round the town: 110
You will remember that the Twelfth was always dry: 20
You would think with so much going on outside: 123